Bali and Beyond

Asian Anthropologies
General Editors:
Shinji Yamashita, The University of Tokyo,
and
J.S. Eades, Ritsumeikan Asia Pacific University

Globalization in Southeast Asia: Local, National and Transnational Perspectives
Edited by Shinji Yamashita and J.S. Eades

Bali and Beyond: Explorations in the Anthropology of Tourism
Shinji Yamashita

Forthcoming

The Making of Asian Anthropology
Edited by Shinji Yamashita, Joseph Bosco, and J.S. Eades

Liu Village: Kinship and Lineage in Northeastern China
Nie Lili

Bali and Beyond

EXPLORATIONS IN THE ANTHROPOLOGY OF TOURISM

Shinji YAMASHITA

Translated
with an Introduction
by
J.S. EADES

Berghahn Books
New York • Oxford

First published in 2003 by

Berghahn Books

www.berghahnbooks.com
© 2003 Shinji Yamashita and J.S. Eades

Library of Congress Cataloging-in-Publication Data

Bali and beyond: explorations in the anthropology of tourism
/ Shinji Yamashita
p. cm. -- (Asian Anthropologies)
Includes bibliographical references
ISBN 1-57181-257-1 (alk.paper; cl.) -- ISBN 1-57181-327-6 (alk. paper; pbk.)
1. Ethnology -- Indonesia -- Bali. 2. Ethnology -- Asia. 3. Tourism -- Indonesia
-- Bali. 4. Tourism -- Asia. 5. Bali (Indonesia) -- Social life and customs. 6. Asia
-- Social life and customs. I. Title. II Series.

GN635.I65 Y35 2003
306.4 -- dc21   2001018442

British Library Cataloguing in Publication Data
A catalogue record for this book is available from the British Library.

Printed in the United States on acid-free paper

Contents

List of Figures, Tables and Maps

Figures

Tables

Maps

Translator's Preface to the English Edition

This book is a translation of a book originally published in Japanese in 1999, entitled *Balitô: Kankôjinruigaku no ressun* (Bali Island: What can we learn from the anthropology of tourism?). When we originally planned this series we intended to include translations from other Asian languages in it, where possible, and this book seemed to be a good point at which to start for a number of reasons. First, it was fairly short and written in fairly direct language for a popular audience. Second, it focused on the anthropology of tourism, a field of growing importance within anthropology as a whole. Third, it dealt with a number of other themes which had become prominent due to the "cultural turn" in anthropology, such as the constructed and contested nature of culture and tradition, the contrast between image and reality, and the relation between successive generations of anthropologists and their ethnographic subjects. Fourth, my own students at both Shiga and Asia Pacific University found it to be a very enjoyable introduction to major issues in the anthropology of tourism and culture in general. The last three chapters extend the discussion to Sulawesi in Indonesia, the site of Shinji Yamashita's original fieldwork, the Sepik River region of Papua-New Guinea, and finally to Japan itself.

Getting the translation into print has taken longer than we anticipated, during which much has happened in Indonesia, and especially in Bali. The terrorist bomb blast of October 12, 2002 occurred while we were preparing the final camera-ready copy of the book. This tragedy highlighted something which had all too easily been forgotten by many visitors to Bali: the image of the island as the "island of the gods" and archetypal South Seas Paradise was something which had been carefully constructed over the years by the tourist industry, the government, visiting intellectuals, and the Balinese people themselves. Despite being a place to which people often went to "get away from it all," Bali remains intimately linked to the rest of Indonesia with its turbulent politics, as it does to the rest of the world with its terrorist threat. The brief Translator's Introduction added to this English edition takes up this theme in more detail.

In the various Japanese words and titles of items in the bibliography, we have used the customary Hepburn system, with long vowels marked with circumflexes rather than macrons for ease of typesetting, except in common name such as Tokyo, Osaka and Kyoto which are usually printed without. Japanese names in the text have been given in the Japanese form, with family names first.

Finally, would like to thank The University of Tokyo Press for giving us permission to publish the translation, Dennis O'Rourke for permission to use material from his film, *"Cannibal Tours,"* Lee McBride for copy-editing the draft manuscript, Neil McNeil for his expertise with PDF files in the final stages, Vivian Berghahn who has guided the book through the press in Berghahn's New York office, and Marion Berghahn for agreeing to start the series in the first place, and for waiting so patiently for results.

Jerry Eades
Ritsumeikan Asia Pacific University
March, 2003.

Afterword to the Japanese Edition (1998)

It is more than a decade since the publication of my monograph, *Girei no seijigaku* (The Politics of Ritual, Yamashita 1988). During this period I have shifted the site of my fieldwork from Toraja to Bali, and started to carry out research on tourism. As I mention in chapter 1, the various chapters of this second book are based on papers I have written on Balinese tourism on various occasions during these ten years. In order to develop these papers into a monograph, I have divided single papers between chapters in some cases, and made cuts in order to avoid overlap. This rewritten version is therefore rather different from the original papers. The papers edited to form this single volume are as follows: Chapter 1. Yamashita (1996a), Yamashita (1994b); Chapter 2. Yamashita (1998b), Yamashita (1996d); Chapter 3. Yamashita (1992); Chapter 4. Yamashita (1995c), Yamashita (1992); Chapter 5. Yamashita (1995a); Chapter 6. Yamashita (1993); Chapter 7. Yamashita (1996e); Chapter 8. Yamashita (1997); Chapter 9. Yamashita (1995b); Chapter 10. Yamashita (1996c); Chapter 11. Yamashita (1995d); and Chapter 12. Yamashita (1996e). An earlier version of chapter 8 was also published in English (Yamashita, 1994c).

Fieldwork in Indonesia was supported by a number of Grant-in-Aid awards for scientific research by the Japanese Ministry of Education, Culture, Sports, Science and Technology: "The anthropology of tourism in island nations," directed by Ishimori Shûzô, 1988; "Comparative research on the social and cultural changes accompanying the development of tourism," directed by Ishimori Shûzô, 1990; and "Anthropological research into the relationship between changes in national and regional cultures in insular Southeast Asia," directed by myself in 1994-96. In addition, fieldwork in Toraja in 1992 was carried out as part of research commissioned by the Sôgô Kaihatsu Kikô (National Institute for Research Advancement, or NIRA), entitled " Nation and ethnic groups in cultural cooperation." My thanks are due to these organizations for these grants, without which the research on which this books is based would have been impossible. I am also extremely grateful to the Indonesian Institute for Scientific Research (LIPI) which gave permission for field research in Indonesia.

I was also able to participate in two research projects related to tourism at the National Museum of Ethnology, Osaka: "Ethnological research into travel and tourism" (1988-1990); and "Interdisciplinary research into the phenomenon of tourism" (1993-95). I would like to thank the other members of the team, particularly Professor Ishimori Shûzô who sponsored it.

In the two years since this book was originally planned, the Suharto regime has been overthrown. In the new phase of history now unfolding, tourism in Bali should perhaps be reconsidered as a further project. Finally, I would like to acknowledge the help of my editors at Tokyo University Press, Mr Takenaka Toshihide and Ms Tanai Rika.

During the course of research, my wife and two children have cheerfully put up with my frequent absences from home. This book is dedicated to them in return for their constant support.

Shinji Yamashita
October 1998.

Translator's Introduction

J.S. Eades

1. Paradise lost

As Shinji Yamashita notes in his Afterword to the Japanese version of this book, Indonesian history has a habit of moving on swiftly. At the time that the original Japanese version was in press, the Suharto government collapsed, and the nature of Indonesian politics was transformed. Similarly, while this English translation has been in press, the Balinese tourist industry has been devastated as the result of a single terrorist atrocity. On the evening of October 12, 2002, a car bomb exploded in Kuta, one of Bali's main tourist night life areas, killing nearly 200 people and injuring hundreds of others. Many of those killed and injured were Australians, with smaller numbers of people from other countries, including Japan, in addition to casualties among the local Balinese.

Events of this nature tend to show up just how vulnerable economies based on tourism are to international violence and terrorism beyond their control. The immediate response from the tourists was mass cancellations of holidays in Bali: soon after the explosion, the images of carnage and grief on global television were replaced by those of empty beaches and bars, and the local people trying to put their lives back together again. Almost inevitably, media commentaries focused on the image of the island as an archetypal South Seas paradise whose peace had been shattered forever.

Clearly the tourist industry will take some time to recover fully from this horrendous event,[1] but the point to make here is that "paradise" in Bali was never a given state that had existed from time immemorial, but one that had been carefully constructed at various times during the twentieth century

(Vickers 1989), covering up a violent history aptly summed by Robinson in the title of his book, as *The Dark Side of Paradise* (Robinson 1995). The first phase in this construction was the interwar period under Dutch colonial rule, when Bali started to appear as an exotic destination on the tourist route for the international elite. There was then a long interruption, due to the onset of the Pacific War, the struggle for independence, and a period of particularly acute violence in the mid-1960s. An abortive coup in Jakarta in September 1965 led to the deaths of prominent army generals, for which the Indonesian Communist Party (PKI) and its supporters were blamed. In the mayhem that followed, Sukarno was replaced as ruler by Suharto, and gangs of youths hunted down and slaughtered supposed communist sympathizers throughout the country. Bali was particularly badly hit, as old scores that had remained unsettled since the end of the Second World War and the War of Independence were paid off. Upwards of 100,000 people were killed, out of a population of around two million. The images evoked here were not those of an island paradise, but of the violence of previous centuries, when Bali was best known for slavery, widow burning, warfare between its various kingdoms and their rulers and, in some parts of the island, sustained resistance to the imposition of Dutch Rule. Vickers likens the events of 1966 to the *puputan* of 1906 and 1908, when the Balinese royalty were mown down as they advanced straight into the gunfire of the Dutch forces (Vickers 1989: 34-363, 171). It was only after this bloodletting in the 1970s, as the state encouraged the development of cultural tourism, that the second phase in the construction of Bali as a tourist paradise began. This eventually turned the island into one of the most successful holiday destinations in Southeast Asia, until violence resurfaced on October 12, 2002.

2. Paradise constructed

One of the main themes in this book is the creation of the image of Bali and the growth of the tourist industry during these two phases, but Yamashita is also concerned with wider theoretical issues relating to culture. Drawing on theorists such as Urry, Appadurai, Sanjek, Hannerz, and Clifford, he argues that in the modern world, cultures are in constant flux, and that tourism is one of the main sites in which cultural innovation takes place. Yamashita's argument goes beyond simple consideration of positive or negative effects from tourism. He argues that the notion of pristine, untouched, ancient cultures being trampled under foot by hoards of encroaching tourists cannot be sustained. There is no essential element in the culture of a particular place that remains constant over time. Instead, culture is constantly being transformed. This is nowhere more apparent than Bali, where the "traditional" culture which the tourists pay to see turns out to have been modified, amplified and developed over the years by a series of remarkable individuals, both from within Bali and from outside. Yamashita describes this process as a narrative of cultural "emergence."

In sketching in the early history of Balinese tourism, Yamashita draws on the work of Mead, Geertz, Picard, Vickers and others. Like earlier writers, he pays particular attention to the versatile figure of Walter Spies, musician, artist, photographer and artistic impresario *extraordinaire*. Spies was at the center of the island's artistic and cultural life from his arrival in 1927 to his tragic death at sea on his way to internment as an enemy alien in 1942. He established a studio at Ubud, which attracted a long string of famous visitors who passed through the island. His vision of Balinese culture was correspondingly influential, as in the classic account by the Mexican artist, Miguel Covarrubias (1937), a book which is still in print. Spies was also known for his unconventional life-style and this eventually caught up with him – at the end of December 1938 he was arrested and imprisoned for homosexuality by the Dutch authorities, in a reversal of Bali's previous reputation for sexual tolerance (Rhodius and Darling 1980: 45; Vickers 1989: 124-25). His internment, deportation and death followed as the Pacific War started. However, the work of the distinguished group of Balinese artists, dancers and musicians he had helped gather together survived. Despite the trials and tribulations they experienced during the transition to independence (Vickers 1989: 160), the work of these artists was to form the basis of the revival of Balinese culture which gradually took place in the postwar period (Vickers 1989: 181-84).

At first this revival was slow though President Sukarno, whose mother was Balinese, built himself a villa Bali and showed off the island to passing dignitaries (Vickers 1989: 3, 5, 181-84). It was only after the dust settled on the massacres of 1966 that tourism and the arts could fully revive, this time under the auspices of Suharto's "New Order" regime, with its constant search for national unity and foreign exchange. Balinese culture constituted one of the loftiest "pinnacles" among the regional cultures which together constituted the national culture of Indonesia, while Balinese tourism was seen as a potentially important source of foreign currency, along with oil, gas and timber. The revived version of Balinese culture was naturally based on that of the interwar period. It received official sanction through the establishment of the Bali Arts Festival, the inclusion of the festival in the canon of national events, and the various educational establishments set up to preserve and transmit this carefully constructed version of tradition.

Even though much of this is familiar from previous accounts, Yamashita makes substantial additions to our knowledge of Balinese tourism based on his own fieldwork. Particularly valuable are his accounts of the importance of training and competitions in the construction of touristic culture (chapter 4); the position of Bali in regard to Indonesia and Indonesian Hinduism as a whole (chapter 5); the economic organization of Balinese dancing and music (chapter 6); and Japanese tourism in Bali (chapter 7). The behavior of the Japanese is very different from that of other tourists, mainly because they tend to stay only for a short time, with the result that their routes, schedules and activities are tightly circumscribed. A few fall in love with the island, return over and over again, and eventually settle there. One of the most intriguing sections of Yamashita's account is his discussion of the Japanese women who have married local husbands and stayed in Bali, becoming both economic and cultural brokers between Indonesia and Japan. Yamashita also provides interesting discussions of the language with which Bali is advertised and marketed in Japan, and of the latest developments in village tourism, as a sustainable alternative to the commercialism of the main resorts (chapter 8).

3. Beyond Bali

In the final chapters of the book, Yamashita extends his discussion of cultural change beyond Bali to three other areas, based on his other research: to Tana Toraja on the Indonesian island of Sulawesi, Papua New Guinea, and Tôno in northern Japan. In the early 1990s Yamashita returned to the site of his original fieldwork among the Toraja, to observe the funeral of one of his earlier informants, a prominent military officer and local politician. He went there at the request of the man's son, an entrepreneur, and he took with him a production team from a Japanese television company with its own interest in making a documentary about Toraja funerals. As the narrative of the ensuring events makes clear, the son who organized the funeral, the television company and various groups of guests all had their own reasons for participating, and these did not necessarily coincide. The politics of Toraja ritual, which Yamashita described in an earlier book, now encompass politicians in Jakarta, commercial interests throughout Indonesia, and Japanese television. The usual power relations between the local informants and the anthropologist are here neatly inverted: the local people are now at home in a modern world of fax machines, satellite television and global media, all of which they manipulate to their advantage. Scholars and tourists are apparently the only people who inhabit traditional Toraja buildings.

Chapter 10, on Sepik River tourism in Papua New Guinea, provides a commentary on the documentary film, *"Cannibal Tours,"* made by the Australian film maker Dennis O'Rourke, and it is interesting to compare his Yamashita's comments on the film in this books with those of O'Rourke himself (1997). The subject matter of *"Cannibal Tours"* is deceptively simple. O'Rourke took his cameras on a river cruise with a group of European and American tourists, filming scenes from the tour, interviews with the tourists and the local people, and the interaction between the two groups. In his own account, O'Rourke talks mainly about the politics of making the film, and his relations with the locals and the tourists before, during, and after the filming. The messages of the film, about colonialism, wealth and poverty, power relations, perceptions of race and ethnicity, and the transformation of local culture are conveyed through the editing and the juxtaposition of material, which are firmly under the control of the director. As O'Rourke himself states, "In the act of first imagining a film, and then photographing and editing it, all my subjects lose their authenticity as individuals and become manipulated characters in the drama which is created" (O'Rourke 1997: 46). Thus, a group of Italian tourists talk repeatedly about the locals as stereotypical "children of nature," inhabitants of a different planet. In contrast, the older local men and women see themselves and their visitors as being from the same world – the major difference being that the visitors have more money, on which the locals rely for their living. Yamashita's analysis goes beyond the endless shopping and bargaining and the economic power relations which underpin them to consider a range of other cultural issues: the staging of a "primitive world," even though in reality it has disappeared; and the role of photographs and souvenirs for the tourists, as a means of capturing this "pastiche" of local culture and authenticating the tourist experience. The locals perform the role of primitives, just as the travelers perform the role of intrepid explorers as they make their way up the river, looking out for crocodiles, sunbathing, and eating fried breakfasts, all to the accompaniment of Mozart. The ludic elements become most apparent at the end of the film, as the tourists paint their faces in local styles and dance, and as the last Americans fly away in a light aircraft, with a cluster of outsized carved phalluses as a souvenir.[2]

Chapter 11 on Tôno in northern Japan takes up a similar theme of pastiche: the recreation of local culture to fit the image presented by Yanagita's classic book, *Tôno monogatari* (Tales of Tôno), and the tourist industry constructed around it. Yamashita's account is based on research carried out by a team from the National Museum of Ethnology in Osaka in the early 1990s, but it also complements and updates the well-known account in English by Marilyn Ivy (1995: 66-140).

Yanagita transcribed and edited stories told him in Tokyo by Sasaki Kizen, a student and aspiring writer from the Tôno region who knew a large number of local folk tales (Ivy 1995: 81). Yanagita published the first version of the book privately in 1910. He eventually published an expanded version in 1935, which included more of Sasaki's tales (Ivy 1995: 94). Meanwhile, Sasaki published folktale collections of his own (Ivy 1995: 89). These tales of "gruesome goings-on in the Japanese rural remote" (Ivy 1995: 67) were therefore originally written against the background of rapid modernization and urbanization in Meiji Japan. An underlying issue was clearly the exploitation of the resources and labor of peripheral regions of Japan by the "center," the Japanese government, intellectuals and industry in Tokyo.

As postwar Japan recovered and the economy began to develop rapidly, the travel industry started to promote the theme of "Discover Japan." As a result, Tôno received an increasing stream of visitors seeking out the scenes and landscapes described in the book. The city capitalized on this, and began to refurbish what was left of its traditional culture and develop tourist facilities around it. Given its isolated setting surrounded by mountains, it also placed an emphasis on "nature," and, by extension, environmentalism, and it became the site of some high-tech energy-saving facilities (Ivy 1995: 115). The planners started to envisage the whole Tôno area as a kind of museum-cum-theme park, focusing on the themes of folklore, crafts, performing arts, and material culture (Ivy 1995: 113). By the time of Yamashita's research in 1994/95, these developments had gone further, and the facilities now included a reconstruction of the *ryokan* (a traditional guesthouse) where Yanagita had stayed in 1908. The Tônopia Winter Festival was now an established fixture, the city had hosted a world folklore exhibition, and the educational activities of the rather grandly titled "Tôno Folk University" were flourishing. The local schools also played a role in preserving and transmitting local culture (cf. Ivy 1995: 131). As Yamashita notes, the museum rather than the old people had become the repository of folk stories, and the local dialect was vanishing. The narrators of the folk stories no longer saw themselves as preserving this dialect, but simply as presenting something which sounded like it for the benefit of their listeners. Thus, just as in Bali, the culture staged for the tourists had become "local culture" for the local people themselves, and tourism was the major site in which it was preserved and transmitted.

As Yamashita argues in his conclusion to this book, it is necessary to view things from the perspective of a "narrative of emergence," in order to grasp the relationship between tourism and culture. Cultural phenomena, which may at first appear to be the embodiment of tradition preserved, all too often turn out, on further investigation, to be local responses to the impinging forces of modernization and globalization.

Notes

1. Despite headlines such as "Bali tourism may take years to pick up" (ABC News On Line, October 14 2002, http://www.abc.net.au/news/indepth/ featureitems/s700457.htm, downloaded March 23, 2003) the industry has started to recover at the time of going to press. The number of overseas tourists in November 2002 was 35,107, down 60 percent from 86,901 in October (Associated Press, January 12, 2003, in the on-line edition of the *Salt Lake Tribune*, http://www.sltrib.com/2003/Jan/01122003/Sunday/ 18771.asp, downloaded March 23, 2003). Since then, even though bookings from Australia, America and Europe remain down, there has been a surge of tourists from Asian countries such as Singapore and Taiwan, thanks to price cutting by travel companies. The latest figures are 68,000 for December 2002 and 61,000 for January 2003. See "Bali tourist arrivals remain strong in Jan," *The Business Times* (online edition), Singapore, Sunday March 23, 2003 (http://business-times.asia1.com/latest/story/ 0,4567,72119,00.html, downloaded March 23, 2003). A useful account of the alleged bombers and their links with international terrorism was included in the Asian Edition of *Time Magazine*, January 27, 2003. pp. 16-23.

2. Both the discussion of the "primitive Other" by the Italian tourists and the scene with the souvenir phalluses were cut by NHK in the version of the film shown on Japanese television.

Part I

Tourism and Anthropology

Chapter 1

Tourism and Cultural Production:

An Anthropological Perspective

With the progress of globalization today, tourism has become a phenomenon of enormous importance. In this chapter I discuss anthropological approaches to tourism, referring to my own experiences. I then present the main theme of this book: tourism and cultural production. At the same time, by examining the way Bali is narrated, I introduce the notion of "narratives of emergence," a key concept throughout this book.

1. The study of tourism

As the American anthropologist Denison Nash has noted, "tourism has become an obviously important social fact in today's world" (Nash 1995: 179). In 1995, according to the World Tourist Organization (WTO), 564 million people traveled across international boundaries in the world as a whole, while U.S.$399 billion was spent on travel. It also forecast that by the year 2000, the annual number of people traveling internationally would rise to 750 million, and the amount of money spent on tourism would rise to U.S.$720 billion (Graburn 1995: 161). Against this background of a massive expansion in tourism, many countries, both developed and developing, as well as many municipalities, are pouring resources into the industry, which they see as a possible option for economic development. And as this happens, it seems likely that in the twenty-first century tourism-related industries will become still more important.

However, in this book I am concerned with tourism not only because it is a massive economic phenomenon. What I also want to look at is the relationship between tourism and culture, for in many parts of the world it has become obvious that tourism is playing a culturally dynamic role. With globalization and the development of a borderless world today, tourism is closely related to the production of culture. In other words, amidst the "global flows" of people, money, things and information (Appadurai 1990), social boundaries are weakening and people are enjoying the benefits of the culture which is crossing them. As this happens, traditional culture, on the one hand, is progressively fragmented, while culture, on the other, is reconstructed, especially in the context of tourism. Therefore, as the American sociologist Dean MacCannell shows, tourism "is a primary ground for the production of new cultural forms on a global base" (MacCannell 1992: 1).

These situations present a challenge to anthropology as the discipline which studies culture. It is becoming impossible to treat culture in the way conventional anthropology once treated it, with the assumption of unconscious custom or a closed system of meaning and symbols. Culture now exists as a hybrid entity which is consciously manipulated, reconstructed, and consumed. It will also be increasingly difficult in future to use the old-fashioned ethnographic methodology of describing a single culture by simplifying and adjusting it to fit the standard pattern of a particular region and people as an isolated island within society. Nowadays, culture is neither an integrated nor a homogeneous system (Rosaldo 1989: 201). As the Swedish anthropologist Ulf Hannerz has suggested, we must now see culture in relation to the macro-level system and the global ecumene – "a region of persistent cultural interaction and exchange" (Hannerz 1992: 296).

Within this context, tourism is becoming a crucial subject for study – along with others such as the issues of economic development, AIDS, gender, the aging society, the media, and ethnic conflicts – if cultural anthropology is to be upgraded (Yamashita 1998). These issues are discussed in the book entitled *The Future of Anthropology* (Ahmed and Shore 1995), in which two chapters are devoted to tourism, including the article by Nash mentioned above. The context of tourism challenges our way of thinking about contemporary culture.

2. Tourism and the dynamism of culture

Here, following the Dutch anthropologist, Jan Nederveen Pieterse, it is necessary to distinguish between two types of culture: "territorial culture" and "translocal culture" (Pieterse 1995: 61). Territorial culture can be seen as parochial and homogeneous, and can be studied within a specific region. In some regions, and among some peoples, cultures exist which can be dealt with in this way, like those of Japan or Bali. One possible approach to these kinds of cultures is to draw on the romanticism of the nineteenth-century German philosopher, Johann Gottfried Herder. Transmitted via the anthropologist Franz Boas, Herder's view became the basis of the twentieth-century concept of culture, and was linked to the concept of cultural relativism. Today, this approach to cultures is generally seen as "essentialist."

In contrast, culture that transcends regional boundaries can be regarded as "cultural software." This approach to culture is latent in evolutionary and diffusionist theories, in which culture can be seen as a translocal process. At the present time, the translocalization of culture is apparent in all dimensions of everyday life, together with the phenomenon of globalization. Translocal culture leads to a situation in which culture becomes diversified or mixed. Pieterse has presented examples of the "global mélange" such as Moroccan girls engaged in Thai boxing in Amsterdam, Asian rap music in London, or Shakespeare performed in Japanese kabuki style in the Place du Soleil in Paris. These are extreme examples of cultural hybridity. They are particularly striking but, in fact, the global mélange can now be seen everywhere in our daily lives. For example, the Japanese wear shirts made in China, eat shrimps caught in Indonesia, and live in houses that are a mixture of Japanese and Western styles. American children are mad about Nintendo video games, while Indonesian children watch Doraemon stories on TV. Here contemporary culture takes the form of a syncretism in which culture is deterritorialized and translocalized.

However it is not necessarily true that culture which transcends a territory has no place. Like baseball, which originated in America and has been transformed in Japan, Nintendo has become an American children's game, and Doraemon has been transformed into a character in Indonesian children's cartoons (Shiraishi 1997: 264-66). Moreover, it is within the global cultural flows that some cultures actually become essentialized. Therefore, anthropologists who deal with the contemporary world in their research must focus on the dynamics of cultural translocalization and reterritorialization, or the dialogue between the global and the local. Tourism is a window through which we can look at the forms that this dynamic production of culture takes.

3. The anthropology of tourism.

In the humanities and social sciences of the past, tourism was not taken seriously as a subject for research. Even among anthropologists it made its debut as a legitimate focus of research quite recently. The first academic symposium on tourism was held in conjunction with meetings of the American Anthropological Association in Mexico City in 1974. Up to then there had been a few pioneering efforts but no systematic research. Rather, anthropologists avoided tourism as a subject. Generally they disliked seeing tourists in the places in which they did fieldwork and felt no particular attraction to tourism: it was a modern phenomenon, and because anthropologists focused on traditional culture, tourism had little appeal as something to be investigated.

The results of the symposium mentioned above were published in Valene Smith's book, *Hosts and Guests* (Smith 1977). This book deals with the relationships between the "hosts" (the society receiving the tourists) and the "guests" (the tourists themselves), and was the first edited volume to address the anthropology of tourism. During the 1980s, after the book was published, tourism became established in the United States as an item on the menu of anthropology, both for research and teaching. In Japan, a research group was organized at the National Museum of Ethnology by Ishimori Shûzô from 1988 to 1994, of which I was a member. Now it is becoming quite common to find B.A., M.A. and Ph.D. dissertations dealing with tourism, and some universities even have departments of tourism studies.

My own encounter with tourism as a research topic dates back to the period between 1976 and 1978 when I carried out fieldwork among the Toraja on the island of Sulawesi, Indonesia. I actually chose the Toraja in order to study their "traditional culture," but from the early 1970s the government started to develop tourism by focusing on their cultural uniqueness. Because I wanted to study only traditional culture at that time, I saw the existence of the tourists as an eyesore. As the site for my research I chose a village which they did not visit, and when I took photographs I was very careful to exclude them from the viewfinder.

However, after I finished my first fieldwork and was going through the materials, I wondered if I had made a mistake concentrating on the traditional culture and closing my eyes to the tourists, just as I had ignored the Toraja migrating to the towns in search of work. For this reason, I conducted complementary fieldwork intermittently in the period from 1983 to 1986, focusing on Toraja migration and tourism. Then, in my 1988 book, *Girei no seijigaku* (The politics of ritual), I tried to depict Toraja culture within the dynamic framework of the wider contemporary society, with tourism included within the field of research. In this way I came to the subject of tourism.

If one looks back over the history of anthropology, it can be seen to have had a close relationship with tourism from the beginning. Malinowski's *Argonauts of the Western Pacific* and Radcliffe-Browne's *Andaman Islanders*, the two books that were the starting point for modern anthropology, were both published in 1922. As I will show in more detail in chapter 3, the island of Bali, in what was then the Dutch East Indies, was seen during the same period as the "last paradise" of the South Pacific, and colonial tourism started to develop there. In America, Ruth Benedict made her first visit to the American Southwest in 1924, and started fieldwork that lasted for some years among the Zuni and the Pima. Since the end of the nineteenth century, when the Santa Fe railroad was opened, approximately fifty thousand tourists a year had traveled to the Grand Canyon region where the Hopi and the Navaho lived (Imafuku 1991: 50). In 1925 Margaret Mead went to Samoa, which at that time was visited by a steamship every three weeks. She spent the first few days after her arrival in a hotel which had also provided the setting for Somerset Maugham's *Rain* (Mead 1972: 163).

Thus the anthropologists of the past century were hardly exploring unknown territory, and the new anthropology which they established on the basis of their fieldwork also took into account the developing phenomenon of tourism. As James Clifford has said, referring to the work of Amitav Ghosh, fieldwork consists of encounters through travel rather than research based on living in a place: it consists more of "dwelling-in-travel" (Clifford 1997: 2). Therefore, the development of anthropology in the first part of the twentieth century has to be considered not only in relation to the colonial situation, but also in relation to tourism (Yamashita and Yamamoto 1997).

4. Narrating Bali

After I had finished publishing the results of my research on the Toraja, I chose the Indonesian island of Bali as a second fieldwork site for research focusing on tourism.[1] Bali is also a famous destination for Japanese tourists. It lies in the central part of the Republic of Indonesia, to the east of Java. The area of the island is 5,561 square kilometers, and it forms one of the provinces which make up Indonesia. In 1998 the population numbered around 3 million. The economy of Bali was traditionally based on wet rice agriculture, but from the 1920s, under the Dutch colonial regime, Bali became known among Europeans and Americans as a tourist destination, the "last paradise," and now the tourist industry occupies a very important place in its economy. Bali is also known as the "island of the gods," and its distinctive culture based on Hinduism has attracted the attention of many anthropologists over the years.

However, my focus is not Bali as such. The theme that will emerge during the course of the book is Bali's relationship with tourists. What do the tourists look for in their travels? How does the host Balinese society adapt to them? What happens in the "contact zone" between hosts and guests? What is the result of the contact? These phenomena form the subject matter of the anthropology of tourism. In my earlier work, I coined the term "dynamic ethnography," which can take into account the macro-level context of the nation-state and the world system in depicting the social dynamism of an ethnic group (Yamashita 1988). The anthropology of tourism is for me a new development in dynamic ethnography.

"Contact zone" is a term used by Mary Pratt in her book on colonialism in South America. She defines it as "the space of colonial encounters, the space in which peoples geographically and historically separated come into contact with each other and establish ongoing relations, usually involving conditions of coercion, radical inequality, and intractable conflict" (Pratt 1992: 6). This concept can also be applied to the tourist context. People involved in tourism have different cultural backgrounds, so that through tourism people of different social status in asymmetrical power relations come into contact. In fact, in the case of Bali, tourism was introduced under Dutch colonial rule in 1906. As Okpyo Moon shows in her study of Japanese tourists in Korea, the relationship between colonialism and tourism is an important theme in tourism studies (1997: 187). Since I examine the history of tourism in Bali in more detail in the next chapter, I will not discuss it here. But I must stress that it is impossible to think about cultural production in Bali in the twentieth century without the framework provided by tourism; both during the Dutch colonial period, and in the years after Indonesian independence during which the nation-state was constructed, following the period of Japanese occupation between 1942 and 1945.

One type of discourse or "narrative" which is common in relation to Bali is represented by the writer, Miyauchi Katsusuke, who visited Bali as the narrator for a program broadcast on the Japanese NHK television educational channel on 14 January 1993, entitled *Nantô ni kieta gaka* (The artist who disappeared in the Southern Islands).[2] Miyauchi had lived for a long time in New York, and had experienced the problems of Western culture. The program was about Walter Spies, the German artist who lived in

Bali in the 1930s. He played a major role both in making the value of Balinese art more widely known and in re-creating it, as is shown in chapter 3. Miyauchi, like Spies before him, presented Bali as the world which modern civilization had lost, praising it repeatedly in his program as a "jewel" of an island.

Miyauchi thus treated Bali as the antithesis of Western civilization: he wanted to discover in the island the authentic world which Spies had seen and which the West had lost. Given this perspective, he was particularly at a loss for words when confronted with the reality of Kuta beach overflowing with tourists. "The people of Bali massaging the naked bodies of tourists is a humiliating scene. Is our magnificent Asian culture going to be destroyed by Western modernity in this way? Sometimes even Japanese people behave just like Westerners and whites. . . Thinking about this fills me with pessimism." In short, this is a narrative in which the cultural splendor of Bali is being defiled by the tourists, and the cultural tradition that the Balinese people painstakingly constructed is being demolished by tourism. It is a "narrative of loss," in which the world is losing its indigenous cultures. Even though this type of narrative is widespread and still very popular, whether in relation to Bali, the South American Indians or the Ainu of Japan, I want to put forward in this book an argument that runs counter to this particular kind of cultural narrative.

5. Narratives of emergence

According to Clifford, "modern ethnographic histories are perhaps condemned to oscillate between two metanarratives: one of homogenization, the other of emergence; one of loss, the other of invention" (Clifford 1988: 19). The metanarrative of homogenization mentioned here can be found in theories of acculturation, especially in those of assimilation. It presupposes two cultures, say, culture A and culture B. Due to an imbalance in power relations, the weaker culture B is absorbed by the more powerful dominant culture A. In relation to the colonial period, this is a model in which the cultures of colonized societies are transformed through contact with the culture of the colonial powers to which they are assimilated. In this model, traditional belief systems disappear, through conversion to Christianity for instance, and traditional culture is abandoned with the acceptance of modern education. In other cases, life styles become modernized or Westernized due to present-day development planning and the progress of globalization, and ethnic cultures become devalued. The homogenization model can also be viewed as a "narrative of loss" from the side which is being transformed.

Narratives of loss can be found everywhere, and Miyauchi's description cited above is an example. However, as I will explain in more detail later, it was through contact with Western modernity that the people of Bali became conscious of their own culture and even "invented" their cultural tradition, as discussed by Eric Hobsbawm (Hobsbawm and Ranger 1983). Spies and the artists and anthropologists around him did not only carry out research on the traditional culture of Bali and introduce it to the people of Paris and New York. They also managed to contribute to its creation at the same time. In short, the culture of Bali arose during the 1930s within the global settings of New York and Paris.[3] Thus, although the type of narrative mentioned before – the uncritical idealization of traditional culture – might at first sight seem to be in Bali's favor, it can also be described as an "Orientalist" stance which relegates the island to a separate essentialized world.[4]

The surprising thing about Bali is not that its essence has survived being corrupted by modern Western civilization and has come down to us intact at the present day, but rather that it has survived by flexible adaptation in response to stimuli from the outside world. What is known as "ethnic culture" today therefore can only exist within the framework of the modern world system, both political and economic. As a result, what we need are not narratives of homogenization or loss, but of emergence and invention. This theory of cultural emergence provides a critique of cultural essentialism as seen from the viewpoint of theories of acculturation and assimilation. If culture is taken to be a distinct homogenous entity with its own "essence," then transformation under the dominant influence of modern Western culture will take place, and the inevitable result will be described as "Westernization" or something similar. However, a narrative in which modern Western civilization and traditional culture are incompatible cannot deal with the case of Bali, because the culture of Bali came into being through its interaction with modern Western civilization. It is necessary, then, to oppose the discourse of "ethnic culture" used ideologically with reference to a "pure" tradition, unsullied by modernity, i.e., an "authentic" culture and a lost "primordial" world.[5] As a counter-narrative to this type of discourse, the concept of "narrative of emergence" must be developed as the key to the analysis of cultural production in today's world.

6. The plan of the book

I do not intend to reduce culture to a question of discourse. What is clear, however, is that it is insufficient to explain cultural processes in terms of traditional culture being transformed under the influences of modern Western civilization. As the American anthropologist Roger Sanjek says:

> Culture is now everywhere under continuous creation – fluid, intercon-
> nected, diffusing, interpenetrating, homogenizing, diverging,
> hegemonizing, resisting, reformulating, creolizing, open rather than
> closed, partial rather than total, crossing its own boundaries, persisting
> where we don't expect it to, and changing where we do. (Sanjek 1991:
> 266).

So, the viewpoint I will adopt is to use tourism as a way of describing cultures that are in the process of creation.

The structure of the rest of the book is as follows. Chapter 2 deals with the characteristics of the "tourist gaze" that developed as modern society matured in the second half of the nineteenth century, and looks at how tourism led to the development of new ways of perceiving the world. Throughout this chapter I attempt to locate the phenomenon of tourism within the framework of anthropological studies of culture. The central part of the book, chapters 3 through 8, is devoted to the ethnography of tourism in Bali. In chapter 3, I look at the beginnings of tourism within the context of Balinese history under Dutch colonial rule, focusing on the 1930s. In chapter 4, I discuss the process of Bali's appropriation of the cultural heritage of the colonial period as "cultural tourism" under the regime of the Indonesian nation-state after independence.

Chapter 5 considers changes in Balinese Hinduism, on which Bali's cultural tourism was based. In chapter 6, I discuss forms of "tourist culture" which have emerged as a result of staging Balinese culture in the context of tourism. In chapter 7, I describe the characteristics of the Japanese tourists who play a large part in present-day Balinese tourism. And in chapter 8, I consider new directions in tourism in Bali during the 1990s.

In the last four chapters, I move away from Bali and explore further the theme of the relationship between tourism and culture. Chapter 9 concerns the Toraja of Sulawesi in Indonesia, chapter 10 discusses Sepik River villages in Papua New Guinea, and chapter 11 covers Tôno in Japan. In all these cases, tradition has been staged, manipulated and invented and it is this dynamic invention of culture that I wish to consider. In the final chapter, I draw together the argument of the book. When one looks from the viewpoint of tourism, ways of thinking that are based on the opposition between global and local, or between tradition and modernity, appear to be wrong. The book as a whole is an attempt to describe the ways in which contemporary cultures are formed using tourism as a means of observing them, based on my own fieldwork in Bali and elsewhere over the last ten years.

Notes

1. Fieldwork in Bali was carried out in five separate trips between 1988 and 1996, funded by grants-in-aid for scientific research from the Japanese Ministry of Education.
2. Miyauchi later included this experience in a book (Miyauchi 1995).
3. In relation to this see the book by Nagafuchi, 1997.
4. On Orientalism, see Said, 1986. However, the reality in relation to this can be very complicated, as when an Oriental like Miyauchi sees Bali as "Oriental" thanks to Spies, a Westerner. "Japanese Orientalism" is discussed by Kang Sang-jung (1996).
5. This is not to say that an essentialist account of Balinese tourism is meaningless. As will be seen in chapter 4, culture is treated in an essentializing way in the development strategy of cultural tourism adopted by the Balinese provincial government. As will be seen in chapter 6, the account of Balinese culture given in pamphlets and tourist guidebooks, along with the version of that culture accepted by many tourists, is also essentialist. In the context of tourism, essentialist narratives have a very basic function. But my own attitude to these kinds of narratives can be described as one of skepticism.

Chapter 2

Space and Time Under the Tourist Gaze

Mankind has traveled since ancient times, but the phenomenon that we now call tourism is a new kind of travel born of modernity. In this chapter I provide an overview of the history of modern tourism, focusing on the characteristics that space and time have acquired under the "tourist gaze" (Urry 1990). In so doing, I discuss ways in which tourism has given rise to a new consciousness of the world, and trace the main outlines of the anthropology of tourism.

1. The birth of tourism

Today, the word "travel" probably conjures up for many people pleasant images of beautiful scenery, comfortable hotels, and good food. However, in historical perspective traveling for pleasure is a rather recent phenomenon. In 1927, the Japanese folklorist Yanagita Kunio gave a lecture entitled "The rise and fall of travel" in which he spoke as follows:

> The word *tabi* [journey] in Japanese has the same origin as the word *tamawaru* [to "be given" or to "receive" in old Japanese]. Wandering around to make a living is similar to begging. The English word "journey" originally also implied having to "spend time," and the English word "travel" is related to the French word "travail," meaning "labor." Therefore, travel was a hard experience. It used to require patience and effort. And the bigger the effort, the bigger the motivation and the decision that were required. So if we look back over history, the aims of travel were limited. The fact that we now travel for pleasure is thanks to modern civilization. (Yanagita 1976)

The early Shôwa period in Japan, during which Yanagita discussed tourism as part of the new modern culture, was a time when the Japanese enthusiasm for travel seemed to be growing rapidly (Shirahata 1996: 3-10).[1] Yanagita's lecture was published in 1928, in a book called *Seinen to gakumon* (Youth and learning), which also included articles such as "Travel and history," "Current Ryûkyû studies," "Studies of regional Japanese culture," "What is ethnology?," and "Japanese folklore studies." In the previous chapter I noted that the development of anthropology and tourism were closely connected. During the same period in Japan, research into Japanese traditional life and culture – from which the discipline of Japanese folklore studies that Yanagita wanted to create was taking shape – was also closely linked to the popularization of tourism.

As Shirahata Yôjirô indicates, Yanagita distinguished between the Japanese words, *tabi* (travel) with its implication of hardship and pain, and *ryokô* (a trip) for the sake of pleasure, and saw the latter as an aspect of modern civilization (Shirahata: ibid.). In present-day Japanese, the words *tabi*, *ryokô* and *kankô* (sightseeing or tourism) have different nuances, but *ryokô* is closer to the English word "tour" rather than "journey" or "travel," and its meaning is similar to that of *kankô*. How, then, did tourism develop as a new form of experience, what are its characteristics, and what effects does it have on our lives?

2. Tourist space

What made this new experience possible were the new technologies which appeared in Europe during the nineteenth century, especially the development of the railway. The world's first proper railway, the line from Manchester to Liverpool in England, was opened in the 1830s. Manchester was at the center of the industrial revolution then taking place, and Liverpool was the port with links to the world. The railway was the technology that supported the industrial revolution, maintained it, and allowed it to develop further, and this technology spread throughout the world during the rest of the nineteenth century. From the mid-1920s, the time when Yanagita raised the issue of new forms of travel, rail travel became widespread in Japan as well.

An important point here is that not only did the railway allow people to travel further and faster, but it also changed their way of viewing the world. In his history of rail travel, Wolfgang Schivelbusch considers the influence of the new technology of the railroads on our perception. With the erasure of both space and time by the railway, he talks about the development of a new perception of landscape, i.e., the landscape as a "panorama" unfolding outside the carriage window. Quoting Sternberger, he says: "The views. . . have entirely lost their dimension of depth and have become mere particles of one and the same panoramic world that stretches all around and is, at each and every point, merely a painted surface." (Schivelbusch 1979: 64, citing Sternberger 1955: 53).

The building that symbolized modern industrial society in relation to this kind of perception with its loss of depth was the Crystal Palace, the site of the Great Exhibition held in London in 1851, the first such world-wide event. As Schivelbusch points out, this building was made of glass and was therefore homogeneous: "The glass separates the interior space of the Crystal Palace from the natural space outside without actually changing the atmospheric quality of the latter in any visible manner, just as the train's speed separates the traveler from the space that he had previously been a part of" (Schivelbusch 1979: 65-66. See also Yoshimi 1992).

According to Schivelbusch, the space which travelers escape from becomes a "tableau." He writes: "panoramic perception, in contrast to traditional perception, no longer belongs to the same space as the perceived objects" (Schivelbusch 1979: 66). Thus, increasingly, the panoramic scenery which unfolds outside the carriage window becomes more and more objectified, emphasized, and refined by photographs, postcards, literature, films, magazines, and travel guidebooks. As the landscape becomes a series of famous places, tourism to see these sites also develops.

Thus the "tourist gaze," as the British sociologist, John Urry, calls it, comes into being, a distinctive way of dividing up and describing the environment. He discusses it by applying the concept of "gaze" introduced by the French philosopher, Michel Foucault, to the activity of tourism: "part at least of that [tourist] experience is to gaze upon or view a set of different scenes, of landscapes or townscapes which are out of the ordinary" (Urry 1990: 1). This tourist gaze is therefore closely related to the concept of "framing" discussed by MacCannell. As he puts it: "tourism is not just an aggregate of mere commercial activities; it is also an ideological framing of history, nature, and tradition; a framing that has the power to reshape culture and nature to its own needs" (MacCannell 1992: 1). In this framing, tourism, through the power relations it entails, becomes a way of looking at, dividing up and presenting the world in a particular way.

3. Mass tourism

Tourism is not just an elite pursuit, but has also developed as a form of mass entertainment. The founder of the modern tourist industry was the Englishman Thomas Cook (Honjô 1996: 8). In 1841 Cook chartered a train from Leicester to Loughborough to take 485 participants (or 570 in some accounts) to a temperance meeting. This journey was a short day-trip, but what made the event a turning point in the history of tourism was the fact that he used the railway to provide cheap group travel. It was historically inevitable that this experiment should have happened in England, which at that time was in the forefront of the industrial revolution. Cook later organized group tours to Liverpool and Scotland, and in 1851 he scored a great success by arranging a trip to the Great Exhibition in London. In 1855 on the occasion of the Great Exhibition in Paris, he pioneered continental tours in Europe. This was followed by tours to America in 1866, Palestine and the Nile in 1869 (the year when the Suez Canal opened), and a round-the-world trip in 1872. Cook's achievement was to take the grand tour which had once been a preserve of the nobility, strip it of its elitism, and turn it into tourism for the general public. He thought of tourism as a way of assisting human progress: the masses should be able to experience it as well. Through innovations such as group discounts and hotel coupons he established the modern travel industry, including package holidays and travelers' checks.

4. Tourist time

The reason why the general public saw tourism as indispensable was a change in the rhythm of life in the modern era. At the start of the industrial revolution, workers were forced to work extremely hard and they were given no time to rest. However, in the second half of the nineteenth century, leisure was increasingly regarded as essential for the maintenance of a high-quality work force. Providing the relaxation and leisure facilities for this also became an important concern for capitalists. In this context, the fact that the first trip Cook organized was to a temperance meeting is of some interest. During the same period when tourism was developing, public drinking places such as ale houses, pubs, and music halls were also flourishing (Inose 1990). The working masses turned to alcohol for relaxation and amusement, but this was increasingly seen as an unhealthy form of recreation, and so Cook wanted to present travel as a wholesome alternative. As the railways developed in the latter half of the nineteenth century, there was a flood of tourists to seaside resorts, which were formerly patronized by the nobility, like Brighton on the south coast.

In the West in the second half of the twentieth century after the Second World War, the work ethic – the "Protestant ethic" that supported the "spirit of capitalism," in Max Weber's famous analysis – increasingly declined, and the desire of people to improve themselves and make life worth living through leisure and enjoyment became increasingly evident. As Valene Smith notes, "the workweek has decreased from sixty hours to forty-eight hours, then to forty hours per week, and for some occupations the workweek in 1988 already stands at only thirty to thirty-four hours" (Smith 1977: 1). Paid holiday was lengthened to four weeks or more a year. Even the Japanese who had been regarded as workaholics moved with the tide and showed a clear trend towards shorter working hours and longer holidays. As a result, tourism as a form of leisure activity became widespread.

Smith defines a tourist in the following way: "a temporarily leisured person who voluntarily visits a place away from home for the purpose of experiencing a change" (Smith: 1977: 1). Here, "leisure" is contrasted with "work" and time is structured as follows: the tourists are released from work; this leisure time they devote to themselves; and they return to work refreshed once more. This structure of time is very similar to that of ritual as analyzed by anthropologists. As Edmund Leach argued, drawing on Durkheim, ritual puts a stop to normal and profane time, and creates abnormal or sacred time (Leach 1961: 133-34). The end of the ritual signifies reintegration with normal and mundane time. Through their experience of this ritual structure, people become adults (initiation rituals), are sent to the next world (mortuary rituals), or move to the next year (new year festivals). These types of rituals function as markers in time.

Based on this analogy with ritual, Nelson Graburn treats tourism as a "sacred journey" (Graburn 1989). In fact, as far as Europe is concerned, pilgrimage, which provided the model for tourism, was simply a ritual journey. It took shape in Japan as well within the framework of ritual visits to the Kumano shrine in the Middle Ages, or visits to the Ise shrine in the Edo period. Thus tourism takes the place of ritual in the modern world. The idea is often present at the start of a trip that separation is rather like death. If there is a farewell party, people express their sorrow at parting and tears flow just like they do at a funeral. During the journey, life is freed from the established order for a short time – the state of "liminality" analyzed by Victor Turner which is characterized by a perception that time beyond this boundary is different from usual (Turner 1976). Thus when we recollect a trip, we tend to

17

say "that was the year we went to Rome" rather than "that was 1957." It therefore seems clear that travel takes over both the structure of ritual and its function in delimiting time (Graburn 1989: 26).

Just as rites of passage bring about a change in status or circumstances, tourism is the experience of a change. Tourists look for experiences which are different. A different culture is experienced on many levels, including sights, sounds, and food, sometimes leading to culture shock. As a result, a trip is a success if a change can be seen in the self. People "refresh" themselves by traveling: they are reborn with a new lease of life.

Thus, tourist time when travelers are reborn appears to be a time of magic. A few years ago I happened to see a tourism advertisement hanging in a railway carriage that made this point clearly.

> In Towada Lake, there is a story which is often told. A girl came to the mountain stream because she was tired from living in the town. The clear water of the ancient babbling mountain stream smiled at her, and the things that weighed heavy on her mind dissolved like magic. "Let's go and play," said the girl to the forest. "Very good," replied the autumn leaves, mushrooms, and acorns on the mountain. Then the girl found herself turned into a maple tree with beautiful red leaves. Having had a wonderful time, she went home at twilight. That is why the autumn in northern Tôhoku is magical for anyone who goes there.[2]

5. The tourist experience

There are two important theories of the tourist experience. The first is the theory presented by Dean MacCannell in his book, *The Tourist*, that tourism itself consists of the search for "authenticity" (MacCannell 1976). This starts from Marx's observation that living in the modern world is a state of alienation in which we cannot realize our real selves. People travel to escape from the alienated world, experience a different world, and discover their true selves. For this reason, MacCannell says, research on tourism is similar to research on revolutions in helping make clear the nature of modernity (MacCannell 1976: 3).[3] The link between tourism and revolution may perhaps seem to be perverse, but what they both have in common is the attempt to recover the authentic from the world of alienation. This approach is a variant of the view of tourism as a "sacred journey" which I have mentioned above.

On the other hand, Daniel Boorstin writing before MacCannell in his book, *The Image, or What Happened to the American Dream* (1963: 86-

125), observes that the tourist experience has become impossible in today's world. Rather than being a search for authentic reality, travel is increasingly based on images. Before setting out on a trip, tourists read the guidebook. They then go to the places written up in the guidebook, and take photographs similar to those in the guidebook. As an example, let us suppose that they go to Turkey and stay at the Istanbul Hilton. Apart from the real Turkey that lies outside their window, their "experience" of Turkey as tourists consists mainly of the Turkish-style decorations in the hotel rooms. Can their experience be described as "real"? Boorstin calls this a "pseudo-event" rather than a real experience.

Thus the tourist experience ends up oscillating between being a "pursuit of authenticity" and a "pseudo-event." Eric Cohen, however, does not regard it as either of these two alternatives. He suggests instead that there are different "modes of touristic experience," and he distinguishes five of these, ranging from superficial journeys in search of mere pleasure to profound journeys in search of meaning. These he calls the "Recreational Mode," the "Diversionary Mode," the "Experiential Mode," the "Experimental Mode," and the "Existential Mode" (Cohen 1979). There are thus many different types of journey, and many different types of traveler.

It is also quite possible that the tourist experience is one that is opposite to the values of the real world. This can be seen particularly well in Japanese tourism. While analyzing the language of Japanese tourism, Brian Moeran points out: "In short, the tourist is invited to do all the things that Japanese society has not hitherto permitted him to do" (Moeran 1983: 105). According to him, Japanese tourist brochures and guidebooks frequently make use of phrases such as "individual choice" and "personality," along with "contact," "play," "light-hearted," "easy," "relaxed," "carefree," "leisurely," and "free time." Here there seems to be a reversal of the reality of Japanese society, with its stress on group values, a lack of space where people can come into contact with each other, and with people rushing about busily. To put it another way, what Japanese look for in tourism is not something true or false, or sacred or mundane, but something which is the opposite of the real world. There is a saying in Japanese, *tabi no haji wa kakisute* (shame is thrown away on a journey), which means that travelers frankly admit that they are in tourist space and time where the rules of the real world do not apply.

Furthermore, today, when the boundary between an original and a copy is becoming increasingly blurred, the very basis of the question, whether tourism is a search for authenticity or a pseudo-event, has lost its meaning. *"Cannibal Tours,"* the film by the Australian director Dennis O'Rouke, is interesting in this context, as I will discuss in chapter 10.

6. The recognition of the world through tourism

Tourist activity is based on movement from one place to another. However, the time and space in which this activity takes place are "erased," as Schivelbusch has noted in regard to railway travel. The tourists sit in seats in the carriage and enjoy themselves, sometimes gazing at the panorama unfolding outside the window, sometimes reading, or perhaps talking or listening to music. Such a travel scene, which is normal today, uses space and time in a way that could not have been imagined in the types of travel which took place before the railway.[4] Schivelbusch has discussed the appearance of these new forms of space and time in terms of their being "industrialized." Interestingly, similar perceptions can be seen in the way that goods are displayed in department stores. As he puts it: "We can call the appearance of the goods in the department store a 'panoramic' one. . . because those goods participate in the same acceleration of traffic which generated the new mode of perception" (Schivelbusch 1979: 183). When the goods are lined up in the department stores, the time and space through which they have moved are forgotten, and the customer is able to experience the world by just being there. In this way, tourism and shopping in department stores are connected at the level of the deep structures of our perception which was formed by the industrial revolution. That is why, to cite Schivelbusch again, the process of putting up the names of towns at stations is similar to fixing prices on goods (Schivelbusch 1979: 184). In twentieth century tourism, "the world has become one big department store of countrysides and cities" (Schivelbusch 1979: 188). In other words, tourism and goods are similar in the sense that both of them are objects of consumption.

This way of perceiving the world by connecting parts of it, which are separated by space and time, may be regarded as the development of a new form of consciousness of the world, resulting from the tourist gaze which has developed along with the world capitalist economy. For example, in the album, *Neo Geo*, by the Japanese musician, Sakamoto Ryûichi, Tokyo, Okinawa, Bali, and New York, the Japanese Genroku period (1688 to 1704) and the present, and gamelan and drums are juxtaposed, rather like a patchwork. This way of constructing the world is very "touristic" in the sense already discussed. In this panoramic and variegated cultural landscape, the cultures of the world are laid out together, permeating and becoming entangled with each other.

The existence of cultural entities consisting of mixtures of different elements as seen here is fundamentally different from the cultural relativism on which the twentieth-century view of culture was based. On this point,

Nishikawa Nagao writes: "Cultural relativism emerged as an ideological critique of the nation state. Eventually, it accepted a fixed model of the nation state. It seems impossible to deal with the different forms of culture in a world which is moving and changing from this perspective" (Nishikawa 1992: 237). In contrast, culture, as seen by the tourist gaze, is by nature likely to cross boundaries as a commodity which arises in the space between two communities. In my view it may be the case that a seemingly frivolous subject like tourism is actually more important than a serious subject such as cultural relativism for understanding cultural production in the age of globalization. We all travel the world, and as Clifford has shown, we should be aware that cultures travel too (Clifford 1992, 1997: chap. 1).

According to Arjun Appadurai, "villagers in India think not just of moving to Poona or Madras, but of moving to Dubai and Houston; refugees from Sri Lanka find themselves in South India as well as Canada; and Hmong are driven to London as well as Philadelphia." He calls these landscapes of peoples-in-motion "global ethnoscapes," which are "the landscapes of persons who make up shifting worlds in which we live: tourists, immigrants, refugees, exiles, guest workers, and other moving groups and persons constitute an essential feature of the world and appear to affect the politics of and between nations to a hitherto unprecedented degree" (Appadurai 1991: 192).

As Ôta Yoshinobu has pointed out, these flows of migrants cannot be treated as homogeneous (Ôta 1998: 14-15). The middle class tourists from the industrialized countries certainly cannot be regarded in the same way as migrants, refugees, and foreign workers desperate to get across the borders from the developing countries. Even so, the appearance of a room in the apartment of an immigrant Greek worker in Germany referred to by Benedict Anderson is suggestive. This shabby little room had very little decoration, apart from a single tourist poster hanging on the wall: a Lufthansa advertisement for the Parthenon in Greece. Despite the fact that he was a poor worker in a foreign country, this poster gave his life some meaning, as well as pride in being Greek (Anderson 1992). The boundary between tourists and migrants is therefore ambiguous, and in chapter 7, I describe the case of Japanese tourists who have married Balinese, emigrated to Bali, and settled there over the course of repeated trips to the island.

7. The importance of tourism research

The word "tourism" often has negative connotations, due to criticism of the processes of environmental breakdown, the disappearance of traditional culture, and commodification which have accompanied it. The phrase "for tourists" is immediately associated with cheap souvenirs and phony cultural displays, a kind of tourism I dislike myself. However, tourism is not only a massive phenomenon today, but it is also producing enormous changes in the very ways in which we perceive and experience the world. Whether we like or not, we live in a touristic world. Research on tourism today must be taken into account, and it is one of the most important areas for students of culture. Increasingly, the anthropology of tourism needs to document the culture which is taking shape within the tourist context. This is what I hope to do in this book, starting with the example of the Indonesian island of Bali.

Notes

1. The Shôwa period (the reign of Emperor Hirohito) lasted from 1925 to 1989.
2. JR (Japan Railways) poster for Northern Tôhoku, August 1993.
3. He states: "Originally, I had planned to study tourism and revolution, which seemed to me to name the two poles of modern consciousness – a willingness to accept, even venerate, things as they are on the one hand, a desire to transform things on the other."
4. In the twentieth century, the addition of the new transport technologies of the automobile and airplane has created a new way of perceiving the world, marked by "the erasure of time and space."

Part II

Tourism in Bali

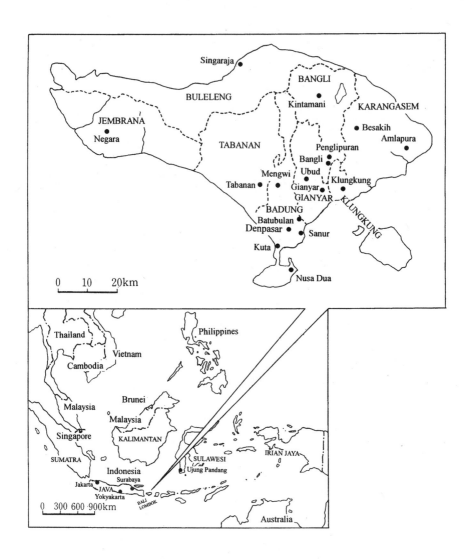

Map 3.1. Bali.

24

Chapter 3

The Creation of "Paradise" Under the

Dutch Colonial System

"The last paradise" is a phrase commonly used to describe Bali in tourist brochures and guidebooks. In this chapter, I would like to consider the discovery of paradise in Bali under Dutch colonial rule, especially in the 1920s and 1930s, and to explore the way in which it was presented under the "tourist gaze." Paradise was not simply discovered there: it was created.

1. Bali in the twentieth century

In his book *Negara*, Clifford Geertz examines the relationship between power and ritual in the traditional kingdom of Bali, and describes it as the "theater state." According to Geertz, the Balinese state was "always pointed . . . toward spectacle, toward ceremony, toward the public dramatization of the ruling obsessions of Balinese culture: social inequality and status pride. It was a theater state in which the kings and princes were the impresarios, the priests the directors, and the peasants the supporting cast, stage crew, and audience" (Geertz 1980: 13). However, as history unfolded from the nineteenth to the twentieth century, the Balinese theater state inevitably underwent a great transformation.

Around the middle of the nineteenth century, Buleleng in northern Bali came under Dutch control, and little by little Dutch power extended throughout the island. In 1894, Karangasem fell under Dutch control, followed by Gianyar in 1900. In 1906, the Dutch army landed at Sanur in order to take over the southern part of Bali, and attacked Badung, the kingdom around Denpasar. In response to this, the royal family of Badung, preferring death to dishonor, committed suicide or *puputan* – "fighting to the death" – by advancing straight into the middle of the Dutch gunfire. Within a week of this event, the king of Tabanan and his son were captured by the Dutch army, and committed suicide the very evening they arrived in prison. In 1908, Bangli surrendered. Finally at Klungkung, the nominal capital of the island, the royal family once more committed *puputan* by marching into the Dutch bullets in a state of semi-trance (Geertz 1980: 22; Hanna 1990: 45-90).

Even though the kingdom disappeared in this way, Bali itself reappeared in the new guise of "last paradise" and "island of the gods" under Dutch colonial rule. It took on a new lease of life, through tourism focusing on its romantic South Pacific image, its Hindu gods, and its spectacular rituals, together with the performances that fascinated Western artists and anthropologists. Behind this new phenomenon of tourism lay the Dutch colonial state. Bali, the tourist destination, can perhaps be regarded as the twentieth-century version of Bali, the theater state, in the sense that the Balinese festivals served the purposes of tourism made possible by the colonial state. In this chapter, I trace the history of tourism and examine the dynamics of cultural production in Bali under the Dutch colonial system.

2. The birth of "paradise"

The birth of Bali as a tourist site goes back to the 1920s. It appears that by the end of the nineteenth century colonial tourism was becoming fairly widespread and that travel guides had begun to circulate widely – the artist Paul Gauguin traveled to the island of Tahiti in 1891, inspired by a tourist advertisement he came across on a street corner (Maegawa 1989: 115-16). In the Dutch East Indies, a government tourist office was set up in Batavia (Jakarta) in 1908, and by 1913 guidebooks were being published, such as the one for a fourteen-day trip to the Padang Plateau (Fuke 1991: 122). The discovery of paradise in Bali took place against this background. In 1930, a travel book by Hickman Powell was published under the title, *The Last Paradise: An American's Discovery of Bali in the 1920s*, and it became well known (Powell 1930). In the early 1930s, there was actually a film called *Bali: The Last Paradise* (Tantri 1981: 15-16). This has been a recurrent phrase in Balinese tourist advertising until the present

According to the Australian historian Adrian Vickers, Bali was the place where Asia and the Pacific came together, and for this reason it was associated with two images: the beauty of the South Pacific as imagined by the West, and the mysteries of India (Vickers 1989: 1). Because of its link with the Pacific, Bali was a substitute for Tahiti, where the local culture had al-

Figure 3.1. Balinese girl (after Krause 1922: 40).

ready vanished because of conversion to Christianity. This was why Bali assumed the role of the "last paradise." According to the Mexican artist Miguel Covarrubias, who traveled there in the early 1930s and wrote the famous book *Island of Bali*, Bali's image consisted of "brown girls with beautiful breasts, palm trees, rolling waves, and all the romantic notions that go to make a South Sea Island paradise" (Covarrubias 1937: xvii).

An important factor which influenced the development of this image was the collection of photographs by the German, Gregor Krause, entitled *Insel Bali* (Bali Island) (Krause 1922). Appointed to the Dutch East Indies as a doctor, Krause traveled throughout the island between 1912 and 1914, taking approximately four thousand photographs of its natural beauty and the lives of its people. In particular, his depiction of women bathing had a considerable influence on the image of Bali among travelers of the period. Covarrubias also saw this collection of photographs before he went to Bali. In his own words, "we had seen a splendid album of Bali photographs (*Bali*, by Gregor Krause), and gradually we had developed an irresistible desire to see the island, until one spring day of 1930 we found ourselves, rather unexpectedly, on board the *Cingalese Prince*, a freighter bound for the Dutch East Indies" (Covarrubias 1937: xvii).

27

Charlie Chaplin who visited Bali in 1932, wrote in his autobiography, "It was [my elder brother] Sidney who recommended visiting the island of Bali, saying how untouched it was by civilisation and describing its beautiful women with their exposed bosoms. These aroused my interest" (Chaplin 1964: 398). At the start of the 1930s, films were made which emphasized the island's sex appeal. At this time it projected an image of open sexuality, in contrast to the suppressed sexuality of the West. This included homosexuality: the image of Bali as a homosexual paradise had also become widespread among travelers. Generally the colonial regime was tolerant of homosexuality during much of this period (Vickers 1989: 106), though there was a crackdown in the late 1930s.

The fact that Krause's photographs were a source for the image of Bali is interesting in several ways. First, to borrow the words of Imafuku Ryûta, the photographs contributed to the "invention of the natives" (Imafuku 1991: 21). Just as "madness," "children," and "women" have been created during the course of history, so the tourist gaze of the Western "other" gave birth to the "Balinese" under Dutch colonial rule. Second, this collection of photographs had an influence on later tourism to Bali, which recalls Boorstin's discussion of the nature of pseudo-events (Boorstin 1963). After Krause, Bali was also spoken of as a "photographers' paradise," and this resulted in countless tourists setting out in search of the island's image rather than its reality.

Another image of Bali was as an extension of India, and in particular, as a place where the form of Hinduism, which had existed in Java before the arrival of Islam, had continued until the present. According to the myth of the origins of Balinese royalty, the Balinese kingdom originated with its conquest in 1343 by the Javanese Hindu kingdom of Majapahit. The Majapahit kingdom collapsed in the sixteenth century and Java was converted to Islam, but Bali was not and it preserved its Hindu tradition. Ever since Thomas Raffles pointed this out in his *History of Java* (1830), the image of Bali was that of a "living museum" of Javanese Hinduism. In the nineteenth century, the orientalists Van Hervel and Friedrich did research on Bali, looking for "India" in the form of Sanskrit texts (Vickers 1989: 81). According to Nagafuchi Yasuyuki, the Dutch colonial government classified the Balinese as "Hindu," making caste the basis of the system of colonial government, and they introduced Hindu law to administer it. In other words, it was under Dutch colonial rule that Hinduism became the "real" religion of Bali (Nagafuchi 1997, 1998).

Of course, present-day Bali is not the South Pacific, nor India, nor ancient Java: it is Bali. But it also exists in the popular imagination in the West as a blend of images of the South Pacific and India. This confusion is particularly clear in the 1952 Hollywood film, *The Road to Bali*, in which the island is depicted with a mixture of images drawn from the South Pacific, Java, Thailand, India, Arabia, and even Africa. For instance, the "Balinese" dance in the film seems to be from Thailand or India, while the device of a beautiful woman appearing from a pot recalls Arabia. Gorillas and tigers both appear from the jungle, though gorillas are not found in Bali.

3. The producers of paradise in the interwar period

Balinese tourism in the 1920s and 1930s consisted of cruises run by the Koninklijk Paketvaart Maatschapij (KPM, or Royal Dutch Mailboat Company). In 1924, weekly sailings linking Singapore, Surabaya, Makassar, and the Balinese port of Singaraja came into operation. The tourists at the time went sightseeing in the interior of the island during the week between the arrival of the boat in Bali, and its return to the port on the return trip. They went by car across the island from Singaraja in the north, and stayed in the government guesthouse at Denpasar in the south. The guesthouse was rebuilt as the Bali Hotel in 1928, and still exists (Picard 1990: 40; see also Nagafuchi 1998: 69-79).

Tourism in Bali flourished to the point that Covarrubias in 1931 noted his disappointment on finding that "the tourist rush was in full swing" (Covarrubias 1937: xxiii). He also described the view that greeted him when he arrived in Bali as follows: "The beautiful Balinese of steamship pamphlets are not to be seen anywhere. The people on the streets are ugly and unkempt, and instead of the much publicized beauties, there are only uninteresting women in not very clean blouses" (Covarrubias 1937: xix). According to one survey, during the 1920s and 1930s, the number of tourists per month rose from 100 to 250, with the annual figure rising from 1,200 to 3,000 (Hanna, 1990: 114). According to another survey, 30,000 tourists a year were visiting the island in the mid-1930s (Pollmann, 1990: 10).

However, Bali in the 1930s was also undergoing something of a cultural revival. At the center of this "Bali renaissance" was a man called Walter Spies, a multi-talented artist who was a musician as well as a painter, and who was also interested in dancing and making films. He was of German origin, but his father served as a diplomat in Russia, and he was born in Moscow in 1895. As the son of a rich family Spies had a privileged childhood, but during the First World War he was sent to an enemy alien detention camp in the Urals because he was German. There he encountered the lifestyles of Asian nomadic groups like the Tartars and Kirgiz: this experience reinforced his own bohemian tendencies and aroused his interest in Asia. When the Russian Revolution broke out, Spies returned to Moscow and then escaped to Germany. As a painter in Germany he painted fantastic pictures in the styles of Rousseau, Chagall and Klee. On the other hand his nostalgia for his life in the Urals soon changed to a strong yearning for the Orient (or perhaps the South Seas), and in 1923 he left Europe for the Dutch East Indies.

After his arrival in Java and various jobs, Spies finally found employment as the Sultan's director of music in the palace at Yogyakarta. In 1925 he visited Bali for the first time. He was immediately fascinated by its natural variety and lifestyles, and in 1927 he decided to move there. After this he worked for ten years as an artist, based at his studio in Ubud in the interior of the island. At the same time, he greatly encouraged and influenced Balinese culture, including music, dance, and art. In 1942, when Indonesia fell under Japanese military rule, Spies was evacuated from Indonesia by ship after internment in Java, and he perished at sea when the ship was attacked in the Indian Ocean by the Japanese (Rhodius and Darling 1980: 9-54). This summary of Spies' career shows his extremely cosmopolitan character. In fact, he was fluent in German, Russian, English, French, Dutch, Javanese, and Balinese, and during his stay in Bali an international assortment of artists, scholars, and anthropologists collected around him. They included Covarrubias; the American musicologist Colin McPhee; Jane Belo, the anthropologist, at that time married to McPhee; Margaret Mead, who had decided to come to Bali in 1936 after meeting Belo; Mead's third husband Gregory Bateson; the American dance scholar Claire Holt; the British dance scholar Beryl de Zoete; the Dutch scholars W.F. Stutterheim and Roelof Goris whose fields were archeology and literature; the musicologist Yaap Kunst; the American film producer André Roosevelt; the choreographer Katharane Marshon; and the German author Vicki Baum.[1]

From this list of names, it can be seen that there was an extremely varied group of people floating in and out. In a word, Spies was the mediator between Bali and the West, and the producer of Bali as paradise. Balinese gamelan music, along with Javanese gamelan music, had already been performed at the Paris International Exhibition in 1889 where it influenced, among others, the composer Debussy. At the end of the 1920s, Spies made recordings of Balinese gamelan music and issued them through the Odeon Company in New York.[2] At the 1931 Colonial Exhibition held in Paris, Spies naturally played a major role in arranging performances of gamelan music and by a group of dancers,[3] as well as displays of arts and crafts. In addition, he published a handbook on Balinese tourism through the KPM, including

Figure 3.2. Walter Spies, *"Die Landschaft und ihre Kinder"*
(cf. Rhodius and Darling 1980: 48).

some fine photographs he had taken himself and a commentary written by
Roelof Goris (Vickers 1989: 108; Pollmann 1990: 2).

How then did Spies try to present Bali to the Western audience? Like
Krause, he was concerned with the world in which the Balinese peasants
lived. However, he came to idealize it against the background of the German
romantic tradition, (Vickers 1989: 107) as is shown clearly, for instance, in a
work entitled *"Die Landschaft und ihre Kinder"* (Figure 3.2). This features
a Balinese peasant and water buffalo, set in a fantasy tropical landscape, and
is regarded by Rhodius and Darling as one of his finest works (1980: 45, 49).
Spies also had a deep interest in the performance of Balinese gamelan music,
ritual dances, and plays. In 1927, at the time of his first arrival in Bali, he saw
a type of ritual drama called *calonarang*, and was very moved by it. In the
1931 Colonial Exhibition already mentioned, Spies attempted to put on a
simplified version of this drama. That same year he was asked by Baron von
Bressen to produce the film, *Island of Evil Spirits*, and in the film he used the
kecak dance, which I discuss below.[4] In this way Spies was deeply affected
by Balinese culture and introduced it to people in the West. His interest in
Bali did not lie in the ways it had changed under Dutch rule, but rather in the
traditional and the "authentic" Bali.

31

The viewpoints of the anthropologists, Belo, Mead, and Bateson were similar. In his paper on "Margaret Mead's Balinese," Tessel Pollmann quotes from a letter in which Mead wrote as follows:

I don't know what would be the best way to give you an idea of the contrasts here. It is the most extraordinary combination of a relatively untouched native life going along smoothly and quietly in its old way with a kind of extraneous, external civilization superimposed like an extra nervous system put on the outside of a body. Motor roads of black loose stones run through villages which are each protected by a magic wall against demons and over the heads of the motorists a screen of pointed bamboos is aimed at the demons. Along some of the roads on which people still carry all their rice – as it is taboo to move it by animal transport, a taboo that is now breaking down – there run telephone wires which connect all government offices with each other. From shady corners where a dozen men in sarongs may be comparing the virtues of fighting cocks in wicker cages, police in smart green uniforms and broadbrimmed straw hats may step out to ask your chauffeur for his driver's license. At a temple feast by the sea, where all the gods are brought in magnificent procession, held aloft in little sedan chairs shadowed by ceremonial umbrellas and preceded by women carrying pyramids of food and flowers shaped into offerings, one will see vendors of "ice candles." These are sticks on which ice has been frozen in the shape of candles and the vendors bring them in large thermos bottles strapped to bicycle bars. And at a theatrical performance at night, while some 500-year-old dance form is being executed, half the audience will be carrying flashlights. (Mead 1977: 160-61)[5]

Just after this passage, Mead says:

But all this apparent "civilization" is on the surface and Bali seems to have learned through a couple of thousand years of foreign influences just how to use and how to ignore those influences. Accustomed to an alien aristocracy, accustomed to successive waves of Hinduism, Buddhism and so on, they let what is alien flow over their heads. (Mead 1977: 161, quoted in Pollmann, 1990: 4).

What the anthropologist is interested in, therefore, are the deep layers of culture and the constants that underlie superficial change. And so, according to Pollmann, Mead drew a picture of Balinese in a timeless existence, without either change or the necessity of change, and in doing so, she skillfully adapted it to the anthropological study of custom, the kind of anthropology which her teacher Boas favored (Pollmann 1990: 4). Here the problem of change ends up being discarded as a superficial phenomenon. This is exactly parallel to what Spies did in not depicting the new landscape of Bali – the motor roads, the uniformed officials, the sale of "ice candles," or the audience watching dancing and holding flashlights.[6]

On the basis of this view on culture, which can be characterized as a kind of "Orientalism," a process began that has been called the "Balinization of Bali," through which Bali adapted to the image expected by Westerners (Nakamura 1990). The Balinese historian, Ide Gde Ing. Bagus recalls his school days as follows:

> The Dutch wanted us to be a living museum. . . For example: when I am in the primary school, I have to dance in the Balinese way. I have to draw in the Balinese style. I have to do Balinese literature. They don't want us to be modern, because that is Western. But we see modernization not as something Eastern or Western. It is the application of science, rationalism. But it is not allowed. We have to be Balinized. (Pollmann 1990: 15)

What the Westerners wanted was not for Bali to undergo a modern transformation, but for the "authentic" Balinese culture under the colonial system to be perpetuated – with its "sexual freedom," its "beauty," its "music," and its "art." As this kind of entity, Balinese tradition became something that could be served to Western tourists. It was probably for that reason that it represented "paradise" for the tourists. However, this was not how it was seen by the Balinese. As early as 1932, Korn, a Dutch scholar of customary law, had warned that the island should not be beautified for the tourists (Pollmann 1990: 12). Against this background, Spies and Mead lived like royalty by Balinese standards, able to live in a big house, drive a car and employ servants on account of the unbelievably cheap cost of living (Pollmann 1990: 18). In this sense they were first and foremost beneficiaries of "paradise." And instead of the new political awakening and social change, they fixed their gaze on traditional culture, and were implicated in the process of the "Balinization" of Bali.

4. The reconstruction of traditional performance

As noted above, an important element in the tourist and cultural renaissance of the 1930s was performance. The performing arts played an important role

Figure 3.3. *Kecak*.

in ritual, in the presentation of offerings, and in palace entertainment as the essence of what Geertz calls the "theater state" – though after the collapse of the kingdom, both its stage and its audiences changed. The influence on Debussy of the gamelan music from Java and Bali performed at the Paris International Exhibition of 1889 has already been mentioned. The performances at the Colonial Exhibition in Paris in 1931 made a deep impact on the surrealist dramatist Antonin Artaud. In 1935, Geoffrey Gorer visited Bali, and praised the Balinese as an "artistic people," since even the farmers were artists (Gorer 1987: 63). Even today this theme persists in French descriptions of Bali: "Every Balinese. . . is an artist, but an anonymous artist whose creative talent is absorbed in that of the community and who has but a faint sense of his own creative power." (Geertz 1983: 52).[7] This was the same image that Walter Spies, the German artist continuing the romantic tradition, tried to find in Bali. Today, the performances offered to the tourists include the *kecak*, *barong* and *kris* dances, the angel dance and fire dance, the *legong* dance, and the *Ramayana* ballet. The performances of these dances take place regularly in villages and as shows in hotels. Since these performances are presented as local art forms on the "island of the gods," their religious and traditional character is in many cases reinforced. However, an important point is that the "tradition" in these performances was newly created in the encounter between Bali and the West beginning in the 1930s. Let us examine this, drawing on the work of Michel Picard (Picard 1990: 37-74).

Figure 3.4. *Kris* dance.

(a) Kecak dance

The prototype of the now famous *kecak* performance was a chorus of men during a trance ritual. As I mentioned earlier, Spies was greatly moved by this chorus and used it in the film, *Island of Evil Spirits*. At the end of the 1920s a new version of the *kecak* was developed by Balinese dancers, with the introduction of elements from the *baris* (a warrior dance), but Spies and the Balinese together linked it to the classical *Ramayana* story and turned it into a spectacle of its own. The *kecak* became a performance by men playing the part of an army of monkeys that helps Prince Rama rescue Princess Sita, and so it became known to tourists as the "monkey dance." Today, a variety of groups perform the *kecak*, but in the 1930s the *kecak* of Bona Village was famous.

(b) Barong and kris dance

This is a dance based on the idea of the struggle between the witch, Rangda, and the sacred animal, Barong. It is a simplified form of the ritual drama known as the *calonarang*, carried out in connection with a ritual for warding off witches. With the help of Spies, an excerpt from the *calonarang* was performed at the Paris Colonial Exhibition in 1931. In addition, Spies, Belo, and Mead carried out research on the *barong* of Batubulan village, and made

Figure 3.5. Sign for *kecak* and fire dance performance.

a photographic and film record of it. They also entrusted the work on the *kris* dance to this group of *barong* performers. In the *kris* dance, the men stab their own bodies with short swords called *kris* in honor of the gods. In 1936 this dance began to be performed for tourists at Spies' suggestion. Performances were interrupted by the Pacific War and the Indonesian revolution and independence, but were revived when the tourists returned to Bali in the 1960s, and they continue to the present.

Angel dance and fire dance

These dances originated in a trance ritual called the *sanghyang*, performed to ward off witches at the time of an epidemic. There are various *sanghyang* dances, but the *sanghyang dedari*, or "angel dance," and the *sanghyang jaran*, or "horse dance," are both performed for tourists. The first of these is performed by young girls from ten years of age, who fall into a trance while dancing to honor the gods. The second is danced by men riding hobby horses. They leap around coconut husks which are burning fiercely, and they walk through the flames. The dance has become famous as the "fire dance," and is performed along with the *kecak* at Bona village.

Thus, tourism in Bali has stimulated traditional culture, and has also acted as a stimulant in the creation of new culture. The two following points can be made about the relationship between tourism and the arts on the island. First,

Figure 3.6. Balinese pop art.

as will already be clear, performance in Bali is a newly "invented tradition." Philip McKean discussed how traditional culture and traditional performance in Bali have been preserved within the development of tourism, using the term "cultural involution" (McKean 1973, 1989). However, the point that I want to emphasize is that cultural tradition, rather than simply being preserved, was recreated under the gaze of the artists and anthropologists such as Spies, Mead and Bateson, as well as by the tourists visiting the island. In other words, what is called "traditional performance" on Bali could well be called a "Creole" or hybrid culture, newly created by the encounter between Bali and the West in the first half of the twentieth century under colonial conditions. Interestingly, this hybrid culture has been essentialized and transformed into the "real" Balinese culture in the context of tourism.[8]

This phenomenon – which the English historian Hobsbawm calls the "invention of tradition" (Hobsbawm and Ranger 1983) – can be seen in the visual arts as well. A new style was born in Balinese art, under the influence of Walter Spies and Rudolf Bonnet. Until this time, art in Bali had focused on religious motifs, such as depictions of Hell, but pictures of the countryside and harvesting or market scenes of everyday life now started to appear (Rhodius and Darling 1980: 55-93). One might call it "the birth of landscape" in Bali.[9] This newly created style of painting is also becoming an important part of the culture of present day Bali. In adapting to these new stimuli, the capacity of the island for cultural reinvention continues to develop today, as can be seen in the emergence of "Balinese pop art" over the last ten years (Figure 3.6).

The second point regarding the relationship between tourism and the arts is that the factor which fostered the development of performance in Bali in the 1930s was the gaze of the artists and tourists who extracted it for aesthetic appreciation. Performance in Bali was originally embedded within the framework of ritual, and aimed at devotion to the gods and warding off evil spirits. However, Spies and the others did not try to locate performance in Bali within this ritual context. They extracted the aesthetic content and relocated it within classical stories such as the *Ramayana*. Balinese performance could be understood by a Western tourist audience within this new framework, and it was reinvented as something that was easy to appreciate (Pollmann 1990: 14). In the next section I will investigate this point further.

5. Tourism as an art-culture system

It is interesting to note that, in the context of tourism in Bali, culture comes to be seen as "art," whether dancing or painting. Here, an argument made by James Clifford may be useful. Examining the problems surrounding museums in relation to collecting art and culture, he discusses the "art-culture system" as a device for creating authenticity (Clifford 1988: 222-26). This system is the way in which the West appropriates, transforms, and consumes other cultures. It is the system by which articles collected from primitive societies are, on the one hand, discovered to be "art," and, on the other, assigned values as "cultural artifacts," circulated, and transformed.

In running this system, artists who discover "beauty" and anthropologists who study "culture" play a complementary role. What is interesting is that, whether in the case of art or culture, authenticity is produced when it becomes separated from its original historical context. Something that is "beautiful" does not need to have a cultural background. Instead, the object assumes a universal value as an example of "good art" or as "a genuine masterpiece." In fact there are cases in which ignorance of the cultural context is a precondition for artistic appreciation. In anthropological research, as well, there is a system of fictional time in the use of the "ethnographic present" that entails a way of reproducing an "authentic" context in which neither antiquity nor the present century exists. Rather than being research on one of a number of cultures from the viewpoint of "culture as a complex whole" as described by Edward Tylor, anthropological research in fact always involves strategies and choices.

The phenomenon of tourism in Bali poses an interesting question for the art-culture system as a device for creating authenticity. As Imafuku points out, tourists, like artists, discover beauty in the difference between their own culture and the exotic culture, and they popularize it (Imafuku 1991: 63). Gregor Krause's photograph of the bathing Balinese women, Powell's *Last Paradise*, Walter Spies' *kecak* and rural landscapes, Covarrubias's *Island of Bali*, Colin McPhee's *gamelan* music (McPhee 1990), and Louise Koke's "Seashore at Kuta" (Koke 1987) represent Bali appropriated as beauty in the eyes of Westerners. As Geertz writes, "most people. . . see African sculpture as bush Picasso and hear Javanese music as noisy Debussy" (Geertz 1983: 119). It can perhaps also be said that tourists experience Bali as the Bali of Krause, Powell, Spies, Covarrubias, McPhee, or Koke.

On the other hand, as has already been stated, anthropologists clearly shared with tourists and artists the Orientalism of the Dutch colonial period. Even Mead and Bateson, who recorded the trance ritual on film were not free of this approach to aesthetics. As Mead wrote:

[I]n Bali, where every theatrical performance is also an offering to the gods, those who wish to make a thank offering or a propitiatory offering can order the performance of a shadow play or a trance dance – sheer heaven for the anthropologist. One of our most successful films was made when we ordered a group to play in the daytime that ordinarily performed only late at night. We had no movie lights and we wanted to film the different ways in which men and women handled their razor-sharp krises in the trance dances when they turned the kris, in mock self destruction, against their own bodies. The man who made the arrangements decided to substitute young beautiful women for the withered old women who performed at night, and we could record how women who had never before been in trance flawlessly replicated the customary behavior they had watched all their lives. (Mead, 1972: 269)

However, the anthropologists' method of dealing with Balinese culture was still different from that of the artists. Mead and Bateson generally recorded events in notes, and also in films and photographs; and in a special event like the trance dance they used a stopwatch. "This brought us into some conflict with our artist-hosts," as Mead recollected. "Beryl [de Zoete, the dance researcher], who had an acid tongue and a gift for destructive criticism, effectively satirized this conflict between science and art. . ." (Mead 1972: 270). In short what Mead and Bateson attempted was to translate the various aspects of culture that had interested artists, but not yet been properly recorded by scientists (Bateson and Mead 1942: xl). Mead's orientation was that of a scientist of culture. However, the version of Balinese culture which she authorized in the name of anthropology did not necessarily reflect the reality of Bali at that time, but was atemporal and static. According to some Balinese, the anthropologists were only interested in culture, and not in real politics (Pollmann 1990: 21). This is clear in the title of the book of essays recollecting the 1930s by Jane Belo, *Traditional Balinese Culture*, which Mead organized for publication after Belo died in 1968 (Belo 1970). "Traditional" Bali was "authentic" Bali with the contemporary historical reality of Dutch colonial rule discarded, the kind of point which Clifford has often made.

Does culture really exist unrelated to politics? As we have seen in this chapter, Balinese culture was also related to the political and economic system of the period as history unfolded. So not only was there a relationship, but both aesthetics and culture took shape and came to be invented within the prevailing political and economic system. The reason for this was that neither the aesthetic system of the artists nor the cultural system of the anthropologists was a universal system that transcended politics, economics, or history: both systems must necessarily have reflected the dynamics of history (cf. Clifford 1988: 226ff).

What the anthropology of tourism really must examine is the history that gives rise to the art-culture system. Dean MacCannell is right when he looks at models of modernity among the tourists, and notes that research on tourism – like the study of revolutions – contributes to research on modernity (MacCannell 1976: 1-3). There are important lessons to be learned from the anthropology of tourism in the investigation of power, representation, and cultural authenticity within the modern historical context.

Notes

1. In the preface to her posthumously published collection of essays, Belo included reminiscences of Spies who "perhaps more than any one person in the period preceding World War II ... contributed to the knowledge and appreciation of Balinese culture," and of the people who surrounded him (Belo 1970: xvii-xxvii). Boon has also written an excellent essay about this period (Boon 1986).

2. The reason why Belo and her then husband, McPhee, decided to go to Bali was a recording of Balinese music made by Spies that Claire Holt had brought to them in New York in 1929 (Belo 1970: xviii).

3. One of the dancers sent on this occasion was Anak Agung Gede Ngurah Mandera, also known as Gunka Mandera, of Peliatan village in Gianyar regency (Nagafuchi 1998: 109-24). He died in 1986. After his death a memorial volume was published by Tokai Harumi and his colleagues (Tokai et al. 1990).

4. Regarding the birth of the *kecak* in the film, *Island of Evil Spirits*, Soejima Hirohiko quotes the following letter from Spies to his mother, dated July 1931: "The whole of this film represents a struggle between white magic and black magic. It deals with mysterious things, trances, dreams, exorcism of evil spirits, and the gods. Throughout are extremely beautiful folk-songs, very pure and great. . . Even though they are not very prominent, there are some splendid looking dance scenes. . . Many of these scenes take place at night. It seems to produce a very Balinese effect." One of the dance scenes referred to developed into the *kecak* (Soejima 1997: 232).

5. The source is a letter to Boas dated 29 April 1936, also quoted by Pollmann (1990: 3-4).

6. This may also be said of a style of picture which appeared in Java in the latter half of the nineteenth century, depicting the "beautiful East Indies." As Tsuchiya Kenji has suggested, this depicted a peaceful and harmonious world, with clouds floating in the sky, volcanoes, palm trees, paddy fields and water buffaloes with youths riding on them – but the railways, churches, schools, together with sugar cane and rubber plantations were not depicted (Tsuchiya 1991: 26).

7. The quotation is from M. Boneff, *Bali* (Paris, 1974).

8. Tsuchiya (1991) examines the historical process by which international Creole (hybrid) culture acquires ethnic identity or nationality in relation to the examples of Indonesian landscape painting and the form of popular music known as *kroncong*.

9. On the "birth of landscape," see also Karatani (1988) who discusses it in relation to modern Japanese literature, and Tsuchiya (1991) who discusses it in relation to the development of landscape painting in Java under Dutch colonial rule. The reason for this was that neither the aesthetic system of the artists nor the cultural system of the anthropologists was a universal system that transcended politics, economics, or history: both systems must necessarily have reflected the dynamics of history (cf. Clifford 1988: 226ff).

Chapter 4

Cultural Tourism Policy

and the Indonesian Nation-State

On 17 August 17 1945, Indonesia declared its independence. Since then, the country's biggest task has been to unite a large number of ethnic and language groups to create an Indonesian nation and a national culture. Within this framework, the Balinese provincial government has adopted a policy of "cultural tourism" in order to develop the region. In this chapter, I investigate present-day tourism in Bali in the context of Indonesian national cultural policy and the development of tourism.

1. Indonesia's cultural policy

On Indonesian independence, Bali became one of the provinces which make up the nation-state. Today the provincial government of Bali has placed tourism at the center of the province's development strategy, focusing on the island's ethnic culture. As Michel Picard and Robert Woods have shown, in Indonesia, as in the rest of the Asia Pacific region, ethnicity and tourism are tightly interconnected, and they are also closely related to the problem of the creation of national and regional culture (Picard and Woods 1997). Here I consider how Balinese tourism developed after Indonesian independence within this triangular relationship of state, ethnicity and tourism. First of all, it is necessary to look at the Indonesian government's cultural policy in relation to the state and ethnicity or ethnic culture. The basis of Indonesia's cultural policy is the constitution enacted in 1945. Clause 32 states that "the government shall advance the national culture." A note on this clause adds: "The national culture is the product of the mental and spiritual activities of the entire Indonesian people. The old and indigenous cultures which were

42

Figure 4.1. Model of the Indonesian archipelago at
Beautiful Indonesia Miniature Park.

the peaks (*puncak-puncak*) of cultural life in all the regions of Indonesia, together form the national culture. Cultural activities should lead to the advancement of civilization and culture, and the strengthening of unity without rejecting new elements of foreign cultures which can develop or enrich the own national culture and raise the human dignity of the Indonesian people."[1]

The note to clause 32 is the legal basis for the recognition of Indonesia's ethnic cultures within the nation-state. Cultural policy was promoted on this basis both during the regime of Sukarno, the first president and founder of the state, and of Suharto, the second president who was in office from 1968 to 1998. This was a period in which development policy was given a strong impetus. Parallel to this economic policy, regional cultures were consolidated, and policies in relation to national culture were promoted.

Incidentally, in relation to the notes on the provisions for carrying out the details of Indonesia's cultural policy, three aspects of culture are recognized: regional culture, national culture, and foreign culture. In the national plan (*Garis-garis Besar Haluan Negara*) laid down in 1973 and revised every five years up to the present, it is stated that national culture will be established on the basis of the relations between these aspects. In other words, national culture is to be formed from the quintessential elements of regional culture – such as the performing arts in Java or Bali, or the traditional houses of the Toraja or Batak – and the positive elements from foreign cultures.

Furthermore, the cultures of the various ethnic groups that make up Indonesia are dealt with as "regional cultures" (*kebudayan daerah*). From the point of view of the national unity of Indonesia, it is undesirable to emphasize ethnic cultures, and so they recognized not as the cultures of particular ethnic groups, but as the regional cultures of particular provinces. For instance, Toraja culture is recognized as part of the culture of South Sulawesi province, and the culture of Bali is treated not as the culture of the Balinese people, but as the culture of Bali province.

As an illustration of this, a Beautiful Indonesia Miniature Park (*Taman Mini Indonesia Indah*) was established in the suburbs of Jakarta in the 1970s with the support of Tin Suharto, the wife of the then president. Here a group of miniature islands is reproduced, which can be seen by taking a ride in a cable car, and the cultures of many of the ethnic groups that make up Indonesia are exhibited in pavilions constructed in the distinctive regional styles of traditional houses from each of the provinces. The name of the exhibition is significant, as in it the cultures of Indonesia's constituent provinces have been extracted as objects of "beauty," as in James Clifford's "art-culture system" discussed in the previous chapter.

The office that administers culture is the Ministry of Education and Culture, and especially the Cultural Affairs Bureau. One of the important jobs of this bureau is to carry out research into the national cultural heritage, or, in other words, to research, record and preserve the "peak(s) of cultural life in all the regions." From the end of the 1970s there has been an ongoing project of recording and cataloging items such as traditional buildings, languages, and dances in each region, resulting in the publication of an enormous report. In addition, the arts division of the Cultural Affairs Bureau sponsors regional arts festivals. These have taken place about every five years from the 1980s. The arts of all the provinces of the country are displayed at a national contest in Jakarta. For instance, performances of dances from each province such as the Bugis harvest festival dance from South Sulawesi and the Betawi dance from Jakarta are presented and contested, and the outstanding performances are commended.

According to Indonesia's cultural policy, these kinds of performances function as an important way to display the "peaks" of the culture of each region. Greg Acciaioli says that this is because, in Indonesia today, culture is defined as "art" and evaluated in line with a view of culture derived from nineteenth-century Western educational ideology, rather than as a way of life according to an anthropological definition. There is therefore a shift from "custom" to "spectacle" (Acciaioli 1985). The result is the creation of some-

Figure 4.2. Traditional Toraja house at Beautiful Indonesia Miniature Park.

thing which might be described as "official nationally designated regional culture." Interestingly, the Indonesian government is by no means treating ethnic culture as something fixed. The "peaks" of regional culture are thought of as things that are fostered by the nation rather than things that simply exist. The government welcomes and commends the creation of new forms which generally did not previously exist but that are based on traditional elements. There will also necessarily be large-scale borrowing of elements from foreign cultures, which will have a beneficial influence, enrich national culture in the long run, and promote development. Historically speaking, Hinduism and Islam are also cultural traditions brought into Indonesia from outside.

2. The creation of regional culture in Bali.

Within this national cultural policy, what role is assigned to regional culture in Bali? What came out from my research in 1994–95 was the conviction that the Balinese provincial government plays a major role in the creation of Balinese culture today. I will therefore explain the mechanism by which regional culture is created in present-day Bali within the national and regional context, including the activities of the Bali government Cultural Affairs Office that is responsible for regional cultural initiatives on the island.

The governmental departments that are directly responsible for culture are the Bali branch office of the Cultural Affairs Division of the Ministry of Education and Culture, and the Cultural Affairs Office of the Bali provincial government. The former is part of the central government ministry, acting as a conduit to the center; and it functions as an agency for projects such as attempts to record the regional culture of Bali province, mounting regional arts festivals, or sending groups of Balinese artists overseas. The Cultural Affairs Office is part of the provincial government. It is the office which is responsible for carrying out the province's own cultural activities, and it plays a major role in the administration of Bali's regional culture. The various local administrations have offices called *dinas*, which are under the provincial government.

On the basis of this cultural administration by the provincial government in Bali, Balinese culture is actually being created through two devices known as *lomba*, which means "contest," and *pembinaan*, which is derived from the verb *bina*, meaning to "set up," "create," "construct," "develop," or "foster." It can be translated as "upbringing" or "training." In other words, cultural tradition does not simply exist, but rather the aim is that of a process of creative development, adapted to the modern world and based on competition. The regional culture of Bali today is therefore not something that simply functions within regional society, but is something that exists through competition, grading and training. As a concrete example of this, let us look at the areas of performing arts and custom.

(a) Performing arts contests

The biggest event involving performing arts contests in Bali is the month-long Bali Arts Festival held every year in June and July, which takes place at the Denpasar Arts Center. It was started by Ida Bagus Mantra, who became the governor of Bali in 1979, with the aim of increasing the affection of the Balinese people for their arts, in addition to their preservation and improvement. The festival which I observed myself was the seventeenth, held in 1995. The organizers, centered around the Cultural Affairs Office of the Bali provincial government, included the Bali office of the Cultural Affairs Division of the Ministry of Education and Culture, the Bali office of the Ministry of Tourism, Post and Telecommunications, the National Arts University, and the Bali Arts Center, with the provincial governor acting as chief adviser. It is a major event in the contemporary version of the "theater state" in which the Balinese people are enthusiastically involved.

46

Figure 4.3. Bali Arts Festival pamphlet.

The festival consisted of five kinds of activities: a parade, a craft exhibition, performances by invited groups of artists, festival competitions (*lomba*), and seminars and discussions. In the festival competitions, representatives of the eight regencies which make up Bali, together with Denpasar City, held contests covering various arts and crafts: from making *pengjol* (festival ornaments made of bamboo) to cooking, and from *gong kebyar* (gong orchestras) to Balinese pop music. The first three competitors in each contest were given prize money and souvenir goods donated by the provincial government.

Before this contest to decide the best in the province, there was a contest to select the representatives from among groups of artists from each regency, selected either through a contest or by recommendation. Teams of judges made up of organizing officials and experts did the judging, while various kinds of advice and financial support were also provided. This was the element of *pembinaan*, or training. It is said that in the province of Bali there are more than five thousand groups of artists called *seka*, but these groups that compete with each other are evaluated and supported within the framework of the government's cultural policy. The important mechanisms in Bali's regional cultural policy are not so much the Bali Arts Festival itself as the processes surrounding the festival.

In addition, the provincial governor has issued official permits (*pramana patram budaya*) for groups wishing to perform regularly for tourists. In order to get a permit, it is necessary to get the approval of a team of judges consisting of members of the offices which act as agents for the provincial government's cultural division. During my research in 1994, I was present at a meeting to approve one of the groups of performers in which the members of the approval committee made detailed technical comments from various standpoints. Approval is granted for three years, and has to be obtained again if the group makes innovations. Approval from a team of judges is also necessary when groups give overseas performances.

Two other institutions are important in the creation of performing arts in present-day Bali. One is the *Listibiya* (*Majelis Pertimbangan dan Pembinaan Kbudayaan Daerah Propinsi Bali*, or Consultative and Promotional Council for Balinese Culture) which was a body established in 1967 with the support of the provincial government. This has been formally absorbed by a provincial government office that was created in 1988, but in reality it still functions today. The second are the national arts schools. These are specialized institutions established in order to preserve the traditional arts, and the education that they provide appears to be becoming increasingly important in the reproduction of the arts in Bali. They include the SMKI (*Sekolah Menegah Karawitan Indonesia*, or National Arts High School) and STSI (*Sekolah Tenggi Seni Indonesia*, or National Arts University). The National Arts University, in particular, is establishing a leading role for itself in the preservation and creation of the arts.

According to I Made Bandem, the principal of the Arts University, experimental arts training has to fulfill the following conditions in order to achieve the "peaks of regional culture," as stated in the provisions of the constitution: (i) compliance with the *panca sila* (the five principles of nation-building); (ii) reflection of the dignity, prestige and culture of the na-

Figure 4.4. Youth group contest.

tion; (iii) development of national pride; (iv) flexibility to adapt to changing times as society matures; (v) ability to be understood by people from different regional cultural backgrounds; (vi) contribution to national integration and unity; and (vii) expression of Indonesia's national identity (Bandem 1995: 122). In other words, art forms become "peaks" of regional culture not just by functioning in a region, but by occupying a position in the Indonesian nation-state as a whole, including the other regions.

(b) Lomba desa adat and lomba subak

Contests and training are not limited to the arts, but are also to be seen within everyday life, from customary law (*adat*) to irrigation organizations (*subak*), and administrative villages (*desa*).[2]

In Bali, the customary village and the irrigation organization function as the smallest units in the administrative system of each region, and these customary organizations have been effective in promoting development. For instance, in Tabanan regency in 1979, the irrigation organization won the first prize nationally for an increase in production of foodstuffs, and became well known both within Bali and beyond. In the same year, a customary organization training committee was established at the suggestion of the provincial governor at the time, Ida Bagus Mantra, in order to train people in the

Figure 4.5. Parade during the youth group contest.

maintenance of custom. First, in order to consolidate the legal basis of customary organization, the committee promoted the codification of the bodies of customary law followed by the customary villages and the irrigation organizations. The committee also worked to heighten people's awareness of traditional organizations, with the aim of adapting them to the times, by holding a customary organization contest. Next, using funds from the provincial government, an annual upland farming organization contest (*lomba subak abian*) was arranged, in addition to the contest between irrigation organizations dating from 1981 (*lomba subak*), and the contest between customary villages dating from 1983 (*lomba desa adat*). In 1986, the Bali provincial education and culture office took over the running of these contests, and in 1988 they were taken over by the cultural office when it separated from education.

The experience of these contests did have the effect of raising the consciousness of the local people. A model for proceeding with the organizational arrangements already existed in the annual administrative village contests (*lomba desa*), which the central government village development affairs office had organized at the national level, beginning in 1969.

In contests for the promotion of village development, things like the spread of water supplies and electricity, the presence or absence of hospitals, and medical conditions are subject to evaluation, as are the village chiefs, the

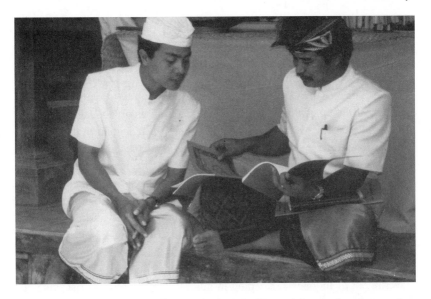

Figure 4.6 *Pembinaan*. A regency official offers advice during the youth group contest.

village councils, and the women's associations. Contests involving Balinese customary village organization include those based on knowledge of the consolidated and codified customary law, as well as the domains covered by customary organization. There are also contests based on knowledge of the concepts of Hinduism, and to what extent Balinese custom that has developed from these concepts still conforms to them. In these contests, a team made up of experts from the local government in each area provides guidance and training in evaluation, for instance, in relation to the codification of customary law. Here, decisions about the content of the law are debated endlessly by the customary organizations, and it is emphasized that the guidance and training team only helps to ensure conformance with the national law.

In guidance and training within the customary villages and irrigation organizations, emphasis is also placed on conformity with the worldview of Hinduism and the practice of inner beliefs in relation to religion. The point of the Bali provincial government's work of promoting, protecting and training customary organizations is to underscore the independence of each organization and its connection with Hindu religious beliefs.

The customary village, which is the smallest unit of government, was given formal legal status when it came under the authority of the Ministry of the Interior in 1984, and of the governor of Bali province in 1986. Moreover, in 1988, the Bali provincial government passed a law relating to the establishment of a village credit bank, an initiative to provide basic financial administration to customary villages. It is always stressed that Hindu religion is the root of Balinese culture.

The Bali provincial government's policy in relation to regional custom has been to set up contests one after another, and it is obvious that these are becoming increasingly prevalent. What is interesting is that, in these forms of contest, whether in relation to customary law or *subak*, the teams are formed of officials from the agencies concerned, and the final judgment is based on a variety of criteria. Points are awarded, and this makes for competitive relationships with other villages. *Pembinaan* is carried out in the process.

Thus, what seems to be traditional culture in the eyes of the tourists in Bali is not an unbroken cultural tradition dating from ancient times. Instead it is a newly created traditional culture based on the contemporary plans and cultural policies of the Bali regional government, together with the national government of Indonesia. Keeping in mind that behind the tourist stage on Bali lies a regional system of cultural production, in the next section I consider the process of tourist development from the latter half of the 1960s, together with the issue of cultural tourism.

3. The development of tourism

The first five-year development plan under the former Suharto regime began in 1969. Under this plan, tourism was seen as an important source of foreign exchange earnings for Indonesia, and ten important regions were chosen for its development. Bali with its unique culture was one of these, and the island was designated as the most important of Indonesia's international tourist destinations. Construction of the Bali Beach Hotel had already been started at Sanur in 1963, during the Sukarno period, using wartime reparations from Japan, and it was finished in 1966. The appearance of this ten-story hotel with its modern facade, still the tallest building on the island, symbolized a new era in Bali as an international tourist destination, and made a deep impression on the Balinese people.[3]

At the start of the following five-year plan in 1969, Ngurah Rai International Airport was opened at Tuban on the southern tip of Bali. Also, in 1971, a French consultancy firm hired by the government with financial assistance from the World Bank and United Nations completed a master plan for the development of tourism on the island. The plan was based on the idea of developing a *mandala wisata* or "tourist circle," a beach resort tourist zone in a place separated from the local society. The Nusa Dua area in the south of the island was selected as the proposed site for this purpose. In order to avoid the "bad influence" of tourism, which was then becoming a problem for local society, its development took place in isolation from the local people (Maurer 1979: 37). This plan was actually implemented in the 1980s. The Indonesian government started to take tourist development seriously by this time because of their experience during the oil crisis when the price of crude oil fell at the end of the 1970s. Starting in 1983 with the fourth five-year plan, they aimed to free themselves from economic dependence on oil, and started to put their efforts into tourism development as a source of foreign exchange. This is why, during the 1980s, Nusa Dua on the southern tip of Bali became a prospective site for large-scale tourism, together with the Kuta and Sanur regions. Luxury hotels, including the Hilton, Hyatt, and Club Med, were built side-by-side in what had formerly been a poor village, transforming it into a high-class international resort.

In 1969, the year Ngurah Rai International Airport was built, there were only 11,278 foreign tourists. As development progressed the numbers rose steadily, reaching 120,084 in 1979; 438,358 in 1989; 1,032,476 in 1994; and 1,230,306 in 1997 (Bali Provincial Government Tourist Office Statistics). The growth was particularly remarkable after the start of the 1990s. A point worth noting is that one of the major factors in this increase in tourism was thr gorwing number of Japanese tourists. The overseas tourists visiting Bali previously prior to this were mainly from the West, but it became impossible to ignore the Japanese, as I discuss in chapter 7. The numbers of tourists from the newly industrialized Asian countries of Taiwan, Singapore and South Korea, also took off. The number of domestic tourists was also increasing, and by the time of my research in 1994 it had reached around 770,000. In the national development plans after 1983 the promotion of domestic tourism was treated as a way of fostering patriotism (Aziz 1994: 96, 224, 312), and after 1988 the focus of tourist policy became the development of tourism awareness among the nation's population (Aziz 1994: 224-24). As part of this, 1991 was designated "Visit Indonesia Year," following the success of the "Visit Thailand Year" in 1987 and the "Visit Malaysia Year" in 1988. The main points stressed in Indonesia were the need to attract foreign tourists and to raise the awareness of tourism among the Indonesians as potential hosts.

In each region of Indonesia, events such as performances and festivals were mounted to portray "the beauty of Indonesia," including the *Wayang Orang* drama at Yogyakarta, Hindu religious festivals in Bali, and Toraja funerals in Sulawesi.[4] The country's staging of its own beauty was a manifestation of Indonesian nationalism. As Tsuchiya Kenji says:

For example, in Indonesia, a film was made entitled "Beautiful Indonesia," and calendars and cassettes were put on sale. In Malaysia as well, a set of postcards entitled "Beautiful Malaysia" was marketed. In addition, drawings with beautifully composed pastoral tropical landscapes were distributed, not only in the tourist areas but also in local markets at the grass roots. The first thing which is important here is that the name of the nation state is described as "beautiful" both in the cases of Malaysia and Indonesia, with the implication that every region of the nation is assumed to be equally beautiful. The second thing to note is that feelings of sharing the beauty of Malaysia or Indonesia are experienced not by the foreign tourists, but above all by the people of Malaysia and Indonesia. Here the matchless homeland, as beautiful as if it was made by the gods, is sanctified, and its sacredness appears to be becoming more and more marked. (Tsuchiya 1990: 170)

This growing awareness of tourism is linked to the growth of nationalism. However, because the beginning of 1991 saw the start of the Gulf War, the promotional year was postponed. It was sardonically referred to by the Indonesians as *nanti-nanti* (not yet possible), a pun on the English "1991." But in fact the year was a success in that the overall number of foreign tourists reached 2,500,000, a solid increase over the 2,050,000 of the previous year. In 1997 the number of foreign visitors to Indonesia was 5,030,000, having doubled over the five-year period.

4. The strategy of cultural tourism

Recent Balinese tourism developed under the banner of "cultural tourism," according to the official view of the provincial government. Wayan Geriya, the Balinese anthropologist and scholar of tourism, points out that Balinese cultural tourism signifies a form of "cultural resistance" to the intrusion of the state in the guise of tourism, backed by world capitalism (Geriya 1998). In other words, when tourism development was introduced by the Bali government, Balinese intellectuals expressed concern that the island would become a "second Waikiki" (McKean 1989: 120). The provincial government was also sensitive to the negative impact of tourism, and adopted the policy that "tourism exists for the benefit of Bali," rather than "Bali exists for the benefit of the tourists."

The basic problem here was that, while the tourists were in search of Balinese culture, the culture itself was threatened by tourism. The question was therefore how to resolve this dilemma. In 1971 the governor gathered together a range of concerned people and organized a seminar on the subject of cultural tourism in Bali. The issues debated at the seminar included how to prevent "cultural pollution" from developing along with tourism, and how to develop tourism without destroying Balinese culture. Moreover, in order to implement the results of this discussion in relation to tourism, three government ordinances were announced. The first banned the performance of sacred dances for tourists; the second regulated the activities of guides in Bali (it also imposed on the official guides the obligation to wear traditional ethnic dress); and the third regulated access to the sacred precincts of Hindu temples. A provincial government law on cultural tourism was later implemented in 1974 (Picard 1996: 116-133).

The most recent revision of the provincial laws dates from 1991, and is still in force. It defines "cultural tourism" in the following way:

> The local culture of Bali is based on the spirit of the Hindu religion, and forms part of the national culture of Indonesia. It is also an enormous potential resource. In order to promote and develop it, tourism and culture should be linked to each other in ways appropriate to both of them, and the harmonious balance between them preserved. Cultural tourism is the type of tourism which can be used to promote this.[5]

In this definition, tourism and culture are not seen as being in opposition, but rather as mutually beneficial. Above all, Balinese culture, based as it is on Hindu religion, is recognized as a resource that can attract tourists. However, the following point must be recalled. Balinese culture is defined as being based on Hinduism, and certainly Hinduism provided the starting point for Bali's traditional culture. But as we have seen in detail in the previous chapter, "Balinese culture" is not really something that has existed continuously from long ago. In fact it is an "invented tradition" which arose during the Dutch colonial period, though even as it was being created it was transformed into "real" Balinese culture (Nagafuchi 1994, 1996; Nakamura 1990). Also, as we have seen in the earlier part of this chapter, Balinese ethnic or regional culture is being continually re-created within the framework of Indonesian cultural policy, through the devices of contests and training.

Here lies the important point in relation to tourism and culture in Bali. As Picard points out, "tourism had neither polluted Balinese culture, nor brought about its renaissance, but rendered the Balinese self-conscious of their culture: thanks to tourism the Balinese realize they possess something valuable called culture" (Picard 1995: 60). In other words, the people of Bali have gone to great lengths to develop the "politics of identity" by appropriating for the benefit of Indonesian tourism a cultural tradition that was developed during the Dutch period, and which became "authentic Balinese culture." "Culture" is the key word in all of this. What this means is simply that the Balinese people have created a local identity for themselves through Balinese tourism. In the following chapters, I will examine in detail how this has been done.

Notes

1. This translation is from the Indonesian Department of Information (http://www.ConstIndonesia.html).
2. In this section I am much indebted Kagami Haruya who carried out research with me in 1995.
3. The hotel is still the highest in Bali because buildings higher than palm trees were later prohibited in order to protect the landscape. Putu Setia says that he was one of the children taken along by their mothers to see "this monstrous hotel" at Sanur Beach (Setia 1994: 13).
4. It may seem strange that Toraja funerals have become tourist events, but here they also function as spectacles. On this see chapter 9.
5. Peraturan Daerah Propinsi Daerah Tingkat I, Bali, No. 3, Tahun 1991, Tengtang Pariwisata Budaya.

Chapter 5

Contemporary Hinduism in Bali:

Between State and Tourism

As stated in the previous chapter, the focus of tourism in Bali is the "spirit of Hinduism," which is the foundation of Balinese culture. In this chapter, I will take up a number of aspects of Hinduism in Bali today, and investigate the ways in which it has changed during the history of the last half-century. This provides a useful way of looking at the dynamics of the creation of Balinese culture between the state and tourism.

1. Hinduism in Bali

During the 1950s, soon after the birth of the Republic of Indonesia, the issue of whether Hinduism would secure official recognition as a religion (*agama*) became a major problem in Bali. The first article of the national ideology of *panca sila* (the five principles of nation-building) refers to "belief in one God," and official recognition of the religions in which Indonesians believe was based on this. Because the Ministry of Religion was dominated by Muslims, Balinese Hinduism had been unable to gain official recognition. The problem arose in December 1950. Officials from the Ministry of Religion in Jakarta went on an inspection tour and asked questions about the nature of Balinese religion: "What was its name? What was its philosophy and attitude to the concept of the single God? What holy book did it have? Were there religious schools?" (Forge 1981: 225). The negotiations between Balinese religion and the Indonesian nation stemmed from these questions.[1] The biggest difficulty was the reference in the *panca sila* to belief in one God, and the question of how to deal with Balinese religion in relation to it. This problem was resolved, however, by the theological argument that the large variety of gods in Hinduism are different appearances of a single deity. In this way, Balinese Hinduism was officially recognized by the Indonesian Ministry of Religion as a religion, along with Islam and Christianity.

In 1957–58, while Balinese religion was experiencing these problems, Clifford Geertz carried out fieldwork there, and wrote his paper, "'Internal conversion' in contemporary Bali." In this paper he described, in terms of Max Weber's concept of "rationalization," the processes of change in Balinese religion within the political and religious conditions in Indonesia at that time (Geertz 1973: 172-89). In Bali today, thirty years on, Hinduism has been officially recognized by the Balinese government as the basis of Balinese culture, and this position seems unlikely to change. During my fieldwork in 1994, the impression I got was that the Balinese regard Hinduism as the basis of their culture, and are infusing Hindu ritual with a much greater vitality than before, within the context of cultural processes in Bali today, and the special features which they derive from tourism. In what follows, I outline religion in contemporary Bali from various perspectives, comparing it with Geertz's account written thirty years previously.

2. Hinduism in the process of tourist development

As we saw in the previous chapter, the current tourism policy of the Bali provincial government is based on its cultural tourism legislation of 1991. According to this, Hinduism is the basis of Balinese culture, and the development of tourism on the island is controlled so as to prevent conflict with this. To put it the other way round, Balinese Hinduism is at the center of cultural tourism, and the island's most important tourist resource. This is because many of the tourist objects in Bali consist of groups of Hindu temples, including Besakih, Tanah Lot, and Tirta Empul; sacred sites such as Goa Gajah; and ritual-based performances such as *kecak* and *barong*. Further, temple festivals or household rituals based on Hinduism are also important resources in Balinese tourism.

For example, tourists entering temples have to wear cloths round their waists. One guidebook includes this advice: "If you feel that you can not observe [the following points of conduct], do not come to the ceremonies, because you will be harming both yourselves and us." Concerning photographing temples and festivals, the guidebook advises: "If you must take photos. Using (a) flashlight(s) is absolutely FORBIDDEN. Use your common sense and be discreet about how you photograph people taking part in a

Figure 5.1 Dress requirements and ban on flash guns in temples.

ceremony" (Santosa 1988: 17-19). (See plates 5.1. and 5.2.)

In my view, the traditional temples and rituals in Bali do not necessarily belong to the realm of the sacred in the Western sense, but in the context of tourism their sacred character has, rather, been reinforced. In fact, as we have seen in the previous chapter, these rules were introduced because of the worries about "cultural pollution" accompanying the development of tourism, based on the discussion at the 1971 seminar.

Also, according to Putu Setia, a Balinese journalist and the present head of the Indonesian Hindu Intellectuals Forum, in Kuta (a place very popular with foreign tourists) the local people have been practicing their beliefs and traditional rituals with steadily increasing enthusiasm in recent years. During my own research in 1990, I saw a ritual involving deep trance taking place at a house yard just behind a hotel in Kuta. Setia quotes the words of the chief of Kuta administrative village: "It is the evidence that the local people now have a surplus of money available to devote to ritual." And the *bendesa* or chief of Kuta customary village also says:

> The existence of the foreign tourists has, on the contrary, made the village people more conscious of themselves, and is helping to widen their perspectives. . . While there are tourists who do not wear the proper cloth-

Figure 5.2. Tourists in ritual dress shooting a video.

ing, the young people in Kuta themselves seem to be more careful about their clothes, and seem to want to show them how to dress. (Setia 1994: 320-21)[2]

The same thing can be said about the performing arts. Owing to the ban on mounting sacred performances for tourists, new genres such as "welcoming dances" (*tari selamat datang*) have been created for them. However, along with these, a classification of the types of sacred performance has also been established, following the 1971 seminar on sacred and secular dance (Picard 1990: 62-68; Bandem and deBoer 1981: 26).

It is important to note that, while the performances offered to the tourists are separate from the sacred performances included in temple ritual, this phenomenon is actually a reaction to the development of tourism and dates only from the last thirty years. Furthermore, this has resulted in a heightened awareness of the sacred. In Kuta, "Western style living has prevailed, and in the midst of disco culture, the young people of Kuta have formed societies for traditional Balinese gamelan music and for reading classical literature" (Setia 1994: 325).

It is also interesting to note the fact that not only do the Balinese receive tourists, but recently they have started to travel themselves. Some of the first places they visit are the sacred sites in Java such as Mandhara Giri temple in Semeru Agung, Sendro village, Lumanjang regency in Eastern Java. Many

Balinese tourists stay for one night and two days, going on a pilgrimage to pray at the sacred site in the early morning. Semeru Agung is seen as the source of the sacredness of the mountains in Bali, and its sacred waters are important for the ritual that is performed every hundred years, on the occasion of the *Eka Dasa Rudra*. Mandhara Giri, which was formally designated as a temple in July 1992, is being converted into "an ideal temple of the future, which may become an important 'laboratory' for Indonesian Hinduism" (Setia 1992: 224).

Wealthy tourists also go to bathe in the Ganges River in India. The idea for this perhaps came from the Islamic pilgrimage to Mecca. Some travel agencies which specialize in pilgrimages for the Balinese are now able to arrange trips to the Ganges. In any event, the affluence which has resulted from tourism has increased Balinese interest in the sacred, and resulted in sacred journeys for the Balinese themselves.

3. Textbook religion

The study of religion is a compulsory part of the Indonesian school curriculum. The students study various types of religion according to their belief, including Islam, Catholicism, Protestantism, Hinduism, and Buddhism, and in Bali they generally learn about Hinduism. Here let us look at how it is taught, in the textbooks for the first year students at primary school.[3]

The textbook begins with an explanation of Sang Hyang Widi, the Supreme God of creation. The earth, wind, sun, fire, water, starts, moon, people, animals and plants which exist in the universe are all his creations. However, it should be noted that the existence of Sang Hyang Widi is mentioned only in some esoteric ritual texts, and therefore he is a God about whom the people of Bali generally knew little until recently (Forge 1981: 229). He came to their attention when Bali was looking for approval of its religion during the process of negotiating with the government. Thus, the deity does not fit very well the religious reality of the Balinese village (Swellengrebel 1960: 71). There is no word at all in the Balinese language for the "supreme God" (Setia 1992: 219).[4]

In other words, the introductory chapter of the textbook is based on Indonesia's national ideology, the belief in one God, the first tenet of the *panca sila*. Hinduism is known as having many gods, but as mentioned before, Indonesian Hinduism became a monotheistic religion so that it could be compared with Islam and Christianity. So primary school education begins with the identification of Sang Hyang Widi as the one God. The exercise in the introductory chapter runs as follows:

61

Plate 5.3. Hindu textbook corner in a bookshop in Denpasar.

Exercise: Fill in the blanks correctly.

1. In Hinduism, God is called (_____).
2. Sang Hyang Widi is (_____).
3. In Hinduism, God is in (_____).
4. The sun, stars, animals and plants are the creations of (_____).

The second chapter of the textbook deals with morals, and the third chapter discusses, once again, the work of Sang Hyang Widi. The fourth chapter deals with prayer, and the fifth with cause and effect and retribution (*karma*). The sixth and final chapter is about the Veda. What is worth noticing is the chapter on prayer where there are illustrations of the appropriate positions for showing respect and for prayer, as well as an explanation of the words, *om suastiastu*, used to invoke divine protection and peace. Also important is the explanation of *tri sandya*:

> *Tri sandya* is carried out by Hindu believers. It is an obligatory prayer. It is performed three times a day, in the morning, daytime and evening. It does not matter whether it is performed at home, at school, or in the temple. The aim of *tri sandya* is to become close to God. We ask for the guidance of the divine light so that our lives will be peaceful.

In the traditional Balinese way of prayer, there were no daily prayers performed morning, noon and evening. This new style of prayer, therefore, is an invention, modeled after the prayers in Islam or Christianity. In the schools today, *tri sandya* is practiced it least in the morning, and the tourist guides explain to the tourists that in Bali people pray three times a day. *Tri sandya* has become officially recognized by the Hindus in Bali. In Singaraja in northern Bali, it is said that *tri sandya* is broadcast from the loudspeakers around the Hindu temples, just like *azan*, the Islamic call to prayer which can be heard from the mosques.

This kind of religion is fundamentally different from the traditional religion in Bali with its ritualistic rules which Geertz called "orthopraxy" as opposed to "orthodoxy." However, "orthodoxy," not "orthopraxy," is becoming the theme of the textbooks instead. Pupils are required to study Balinese religion at school, and during the time for religious studies, knowledge is tested by questions such as "What is *trimurti*?" Or "What are *pura desa*, *pura puseh*, and *pura dalem* called?" This marks a shift in emphasis from practice to doctrine in religious learning.

Furthermore, at bookshops in Denpasar a variety of books on Hinduism are on sale, ranging from explanations of doctrine to the way to perform ritual and make decorations. People not only learn about Hinduism in schools, but also from a range of these publications. Certainly, writings on religion in Bali are not necessarily recent. There were once traditional writings on palmyra leaves (*lontara*) which provided esoteric knowledge which was limited to special groups and families like the Brahmins. In contrast, the present publications are printed in large numbers, and are available to everyone. In this regard, they are completely different from the old palmyra documents. The bookshops also sell posters with images of the gods like those of Indian Hinduism, regardless of the fact that one feature of Balinese Hinduism was that it did not use the Indian images which were different from its own.

Geertz once described Balinese religion in the following way:

> Beyond a minimal level, there is almost no interest in doctrine, or generalized interpretation of what is going on, at all. . . the worshippers usually don't even know who the gods in the temples are, are uninterested in the meaning of the rich symbolism, and are indifferent to what others may or may not believe. (Geertz 1973: 177)

However, what I have said so far makes it clear that we have to update Geertz's observations. The Balinese anthropologist, Ngrah Bagus, also says that Hinduism today has to address many problems, such as development and poverty, backwardness and fatalism, and education, so it is no longer a religion which is preoccupied with ritual alone (Bagus 1992).

4. Ritual clothing

I have already mentioned the young people of Kuta whose response to tourists inappropriately dressed for rituals is: "we ourselves are careful about our clothes, and we want to show you how to dress properly." In my research during 1994–95, one thing that impressed me very much was the clothes of the Balinese, especially what they wore during rituals.[5] Ritual clothing, which was relatively unstandardized before, is now highly standardized. At times of festivals in the temples, the men wear white headcloths, white clothes, and over their loincloths (which are of no fixed color) they wear a yellow *kampuh* (cover cloth). The women wear *kebaya* (a long-sleeved blouse – the color is not specified but is often yellow), with a white waistcloth. For funerals they wear black.

During Balinese festivals, men and women, adults and children, old and young all put on makeup. Even men who usually dress carelessly wear headcloths, and these create a colorful effect along with the flowers piled around their ears. People also wear high quality clothes. Bali currently has the highest incomes in Indonesia after Jakarta, and above all the Balinese like to put their money into clothes for festivals. In particular, rich people of high status wear expensive clothes with gold embroidery.

This attention to dress is not limited to the traditional ritual setting. In the government assembly as well, Indonesian formal clothes made out of batik or ikat are becoming de rigueur, and Bali-style dress is also becoming necessary on some occasions. During my research in 1995, I had a chance to participate in contests by the state government culture office, such as *lomba desa adat* (the traditional village contest), *lomba subak abian* (the dry field farming contest), and *lomba seka terna* (the youth group contest). In these contests, people are required to dress the same way as they would for a temple festival, and the clothes worn during these contests are themselves subject to evaluation. Also, a variety of competitions are held during the Balinese arts festivals discussed in the previous chapter, and some of those are for traditional dress.

One more theme which emerged during the course of my research was the use of black for funeral clothing. As already indicated, black clothes are worn for funerals today. However, according to the *Bali Post*, the local Balinese newspaper, the regulation color of funeral clothes in Hinduism is not really black, so present-day practice seems to be the result of Western influence.[6]

Balinese traditional clothes (*busana adat*), are divided into the three following categories: (i) formal clothing (*busana agung adat*); (ii) traditional work clothes (*busana adat reresonan*); and (iii) modern customary dress (*busana adat modern*) (Sugriwa 1991: 46-52). The first of these categories consists of expensive clothes, made with gold or silver, and the local term literally means "big clothes." Today, these are used at the tooth sharpening ceremony marking adulthood, and at weddings. When they are used, shirts are not worn, and men wear a ritual sword behind. The headcloth is also made with cloth woven with gold. The women wear golden earrings woven with flowers. The second category consists of loin cloths and cloths covering the chest, or nowadays shirts. In the third category, the men wear loin cloths, shirts or jackets, and *kampuh*, and the women wear loin cloths and waistcloths with a *kebaya*. Men's jackets recall the palace or military dress during the colonial period. The women's *kebaya* was originally based on women's dress in Java, and now it is widely used throughout Indonesia. For this reason, "modern" here is equated with "Indonesian."

In many places in the world, clothing is an important symbol of ethnic identity. What is interesting here is the point that regulations governing the use of clothing in rituals and festivals in contemporary Bali have been strengthened, especially in relation to "modern customary clothing" of the three categories mentioned above. Since "modern" could well be described as "Indonesian," the strengthening of these regulations actually emphasizes Bali's position as part of Indonesia.

5. The influence of urbanization

As economic development has progressed in Indonesia, so has urbanization. The urban population as a percentage of the total population has increased from around 15 percent in 1961 to around 31 percent in 1991. In parallel with this trend, the people of Bali have also left the countryside for the city in search of education and work. What form, then, has Hinduism taken in the cities as people with different backgrounds have become concentrated there? As an example, one person whom I know, Mr. W., works as a dentist in Denpasar. For him, Denpasar is nothing but a work place, though his home area is Negara in Jembrana regency in western Bali. He is not involved in any religious activities in Denpasar, and he goes back to his own rural area for rituals and festivals. From Denpasar to Negara is around two hours by car, and Mr W. regularly spends the weekends in the country. This is possible if the distance to the countryside allows one to return frequently, but the Balinese who have gone to Jakarta cannot go back to Bali so often. So what kind of religious life is possible for them?

Kagami has discussed this question (Kagami 1992: 326-27). According to him, the Hindu population of Jakarta in 1990 was about 52,846, with sixteen Hindu temples. In fact, in addition to the Balinese, the "Hindus" included people of Indian descent, Sikhs, Kaharingan believers from Kalimantan, and Aluk To Dolo followers from Tana Toraja, in addition to peoples such as the Karo Batak, the Tenger from Java, the Badui from Western Java, and the Kejawen from Central Java. In other words, Hinduism is not restricted to Bali and there are Hindu communities beyond.[7]

According to Kagami, the Hindu temples in Jakarta and the activities there are different from those in Bali in the following ways. First, the shrines for the worship of the high god are set up in the center of the inner sanctuary, and this is different from the traditional pattern in Bali where the central position is given to the god of the temple. Second, the rituals for the full moon and the new moon are carried out at fixed times, which is not the case in Bali. Third, it is common for devout people to offer prayers three times a day (*tri sandya*), at sunrise, noon and sunset, either at home or at work. So practicing Hinduism in Jakarta is becoming more a matter of doctrine and principle (Kagami 1992: 326-27).

These trends are also happening in Bali itself, at the Jagadnatha temple in Denpasar, the temple built by the Parisada in the 1960s. (Parisada is the Indonesian Hindu Congress, founded in 1957, and the group which has been promoting the rationalization of Balinese and Indonesian Hinduism.) In the center of this temple is the seat of Sang Hyang Widi, and in addition to the normal festival days, rituals are also carried out on the days of the full moon and the new moon. On these occasions people chant the sutras over and over again, followed by sermons from the priests. When compared with the traditional style of ritual in Bali, this appears very different (Forge 1981: 229). At first only officials from the Parisada and their disciples took part in these activities, but now the number of general participants is increasing. At the prayers for the full moon and new moon, the younger generation is particularly involved. A temple like Jagadnatha is also being built at Singaraja, and others are planned at Amlapura in Karangasem regency, and at Negara in Jembrana regency. What is also interesting is that where Hindu temples are being built outside Bali, generally it is the Jagadnatha style of temple which is constructed (*Bali Post*, 12 October 1994).

One further point of interest in Kagami's account is that in Jakarta, custom is stressed much less than religion. In particular, the ordinary clothing for prayers generally consists simply of a cloth wrapped round a person's waist, and there are few people dressed in the kind of uniform found in Bali. The reason is that, in Jakarta, people see as inappropriate clothes that they would wear in Bali (Kagami 1992: 327). This is in sharp contrast to Bali itself, where people take a great interest in dress on ritual occasions, as ritual itself becomes increasingly magnificent.

In the temples in Jakarta, there are educational activities including a Sunday School, in addition to the ritual. In Bali, Hinduism is taught during religious studies classes at school, but in Jakarta, where there are many Muslims, religious studies at school consist of classes on Islam. Putu Setia talks about the religion of his children's generation:

Rini and Wirya, my two children, are being brought up in the Javanese environment, they speak Javanese, they have lots of friends in the mosques and the churches, and they are learning about Hinduism at the Rawamangun temple in Jakarta. With this kind of religious education, they have little contact with their parents' generation. The younger generation know about religion, but they do not know anything about the kind of ritual in Bali. They will probably end up like Rini and Wirya. (Setia 1994: 22-23)

6. From orthopraxy to orthodoxy

In his paper internal conversion, Geertz wrote as follows: "What will come of all this – the intensified religious questioning, the spread of religious literacy, and the attempt to reorganize religious institutions – remains to be seen" (Geertz 1973: 189). Now, thirty years after this paper was written, how exactly has religious practice turned out? So far I have provided a sketch based on my own research of aspects of contemporary Hinduism taking shape in Bali, and I will address this question based on these observations.

To summarize the changes in Balinese religion discussed up to now, the main point to be emphasized is the shift from orthopraxy to orthodoxy. In part, this shift has been brought about by the Parisada campaign to reform Hinduism. But rather than being simply the result of this campaign, the changes seem to be accelerating within the social, economic, and cultural circumstances surrounding Balinese society today. As Indonesia's development policy progressed, tourism continued to develop, resulting in the visits by a large number of tourists. On the other hand, the contemporary social situation in Bali is that the Balinese themselves are leaving the island in all directions in search of work and education. Against this background, religion is increasingly unable to perform its role in the way it once did. According to Forge, what Parisada did was to rationalize the Balinese religion, which was based on the cooperative worship of ancestors and gods, and therefore was difficult to transplant so as to benefit people who had no local ancestors or gods (Forge 1981: 226-27). In other words, Parisada "deterritorialized" Hinduism. This is probably why it had greater success outside Bali than on the island itself.

The deterritorialization of religion is also becoming an increasingly real problem for Bali today. The important role of books and doctrine in current Balinese Hinduism can be understood in the light of this. Books and doctrines are both portable, and they are more likely to be used by individuals separated from their communities than by people within their communities. As Fukushima Masato has suggested (1991: 117), this means that, rather than looking at changes in Balinese religion using Weber's model of rationalization as Geertz does, it is more persuasive to see changes as a shift towards ideas of salvation, as a result of the shift away from communal religions towards individualism and religious doctrine. The significance of this strengthening of orthodoxy at the expense of orthopraxy can be understood precisely in this transition. In fact, what seems to be emerging – along with the religious lessons in primary school, the increasing number of publications on Hinduism, and the resulting stress on doctrine rather than custom among urban Hindus – is not so much a process of secularization or rationalization, following Weber and Geertz, but rather a new religious consciousness based on the individualistic beliefs that go together with economic development and urbanization.[8]

However, it must quickly be added that Balinese ritualism certainly does not seem to be on the way out. Rather, as noted before, the development of tourism has strengthened Hindu spirituality, and the performance of ritual is actually flourishing. The meaning of this, as James Boon has already suggested, is that in Bali the rationalization of religion and the strengthening of ritualism are actually not in opposition to each other: rather they can exist together as is more or less the case here (Boon 1979: 288-89). The Balinese ritualism which Geertz discussed thirty years ago can still be seen, even today: "The Balinese, perpetually weaving intricate palm-leaf offerings, preparing elaborate ritual meals, decorating all sorts of temples, marching in massive processions, and falling into sudden trances, seem much too busy practicing their religion to think (or worry) very much about it" (Geertz 1973: 176).

However, behind this visible exterior are Balinese who are thinking and worrying about their religion. Putu Setia describes the following episode. His two children went to a Catholic school in Jakarta, and they were once asked by a teacher whether or not they prayed before meals in Hinduism. The children did not answer and stayed silent, but another student answered: "There is no prayer, teacher, but the Hindus make offerings to the evil spirits before a meal." So Setia's children asked Setia himself: "Why are there no prayers before a meal in Hinduism?" Setia then recited prayers before meals in Sanskrit from the collection of prayers written by Adia Wirattmadja. He also said that there are prayers to be used before starting a meal, and prayers for use after it. But the children protested that it was very difficult to remember prayers in Sanskrit. Setia answered: "If you can, use prayers in their original language. At first, praying three times a day seems difficult, but when you get used to it, it is probably not difficult. But if you cannot, it is all right to use a language you can manage, like Indonesian [his children could not speak Balinese]" (Setia, 1992: 211-12). This is an episode from a Balinese family in Jakarta. However, similar things can be seen in Bali as society becomes more fluid. Even though Balinese ritualism continues, it is not unconscious "custom" embedded in the society but custom that is being consciously manipulated and created within the wider social, cultural, and economic context.

7. Is the essence changing?

The anthropologist Yoshida Teigo, one of the pioneer Japanese researchers on Bali, has written as follows:

> From the autumn of 1974 to the beginning of the following year I observed Balinese culture and especially its religion. Seventeen years later (in the spring and summer of 1991), when I went back and compared it, things remained the same in spite of the campaign to rationalize Balinese religion. Namely, in the case of the funerals (burials) and cremations that I saw, I thought that there was no essential change in spite of the remarkable growth of tourism, and the Balinese said that they thought the same. I thought that the flood of tourist development and modernization, rather

than changing Balinese culture, was actually acting to perpetuate and strengthen it. (Yoshida 1994: 157)

Similar observations – that visible changes are superficial and the essence remains the same – were also made by Margaret Mead, who carried out research in Bali sixty years before, as we have seen in chapter 3 (Mead 1977: 160-62). However, when ethnologists say "there is no essential change," it may be that this is an ideology which essentializes culture. The conventional way of dealing with this kind of culture is to depict it as a "deep layer" of "traditional" culture. This means that by emphasizing the "unchanging substance" of culture, the ethnologists are helping to essentialize it.[9]

Morris Bloch investigated the changes in ritual over 200 years of history among the Merina of Madagascar, and pointed out that the propositions that ritual had changed and ritual had not changed were both true at the same time. He said that this is a problem related to the substance of ideology (Bloch 1986). However, the problem with Bloch's position is that behind the mask of continuity of tradition, the consciousness which underlies it may change drastically from within. As culture changes from unconscious custom to manipulated symbol, the relationship between the surface layer and deep layer, i.e. between change and essence, is reversed. The ironic result is that beneath the superficial continuity the essence is secretly being transformed. The key concept here, therefore, is not "Balinese culture" but "Balinese simulation." I will return to this point in chapter 11, when I consider the case of tourism in Tôno, in Iwate prefecture, Japan.

Notes

1. Jane Atkinson describes the relations between traditional religion and the Indonesian state for the Wana of Central Sulawesi as "religions in dialogue" (Atkinson 1983). However, in the Balinese case it involved political discussions with the state over legal status, so that "negotiations" might be more appropriate than "dialogue."
2. Balinese villages are divided into administrative villages, *desa dinas*, which are the basic units of government administration, and customary villages, *desa adat*, which are the basic units for customary law.
3. The textbook used here is *Penuntun Belajar Agama Hindu 1* (Berdsarkan kurikulum baru GBPP 1994), published by Ganeca Exact Bandung Company.
4. Here "One God" is translated using the Indonesian word *Tuhan*.

5. Kagami has discussed this in his 1995 paper. The 1994–95 research was a joint project we carried out together, and here I share many of Kagami's observations.

6. *Bali Post*, 19 October 1994. The same kind of thing can be said about the Toraja of Sulawesi. On the occasion of Toraja funerals clothing was formerly not necessarily black, but in recent years the use of black has become common.

7. Of Indonesia's Hindus, 93.3 percent live in Bali, while the other 6.7 percent live outside (Bagus, 1992: 55). The relationship between Hinduism and other belief systems such as ancestor worship among the Kaharingan of Kalimantan, the Aluk to Dolo' of the Toraja, Tenger religion, and Javanese animism are discussed by Fukushima (1991: 119-54). In relation to the Hindu revival in Java in the 1970s, see Lyon (1980).

8. In his summary of the trend towards higher forms of Buddhism in Thailand and Sri Lanka from the 1970s, Tanabe Shigeharu (1993) discusses the new forms of religion that have accompanied economic development and urbanization.

9. In relation to the critique of cultural essentialism, see Ôta (1998: chapter 4). He makes the point that in the aboriginal movements in Hawaii and among the Maya of Guatamala in which he has most recently been interested, the local people are empowered by an essentialist ideology. When movements are thus based, the anthropologist is at a loss as to how to approach them. There is no general answer to this problem. I do not say that essentializing culture is necessarily wrong. It varies according to the context.

Chapter 6

Staging Paradise: The Development of

Touristic Culture

In the contact zone between "hosts" and "guests," culture is staged for the purposes of tourism, and the result is the development of what might be called "touristic culture." In this chapter I want to shed light on the cultural dynamics of this zone, and explore the way "paradise" is staged in Balinese tourism, together with the way touristic culture is created.

1. The image of Bali

As Yamanaka Hayato points out, in order to establish tourism, the image of the target region has to be systematically produced and disseminated (Yamanaka 1992: 213). The contemporary media have taken on a major role in making these kinds of images available. Before tourists set out on their tours they read pamphlets and guidebooks, and they first grasp the image of the place they are bound for. How are, then, tourist images of Indonesia and Bali presented in the advertising copy in tourist pamphlets?

Indonesia is a country which is said to be a unity of diversity, a country of around 13,000 islands with their varied and vibrant cultures. Typical are the island of Bali with its gods, festivals and beaches, and the ancient site of Borobudur. It is also a country overflowing with spices and fruits.[1]

Take for instance Borobudur. Who built what is said to be the largest and oldest Buddhist temple in the world, and why? Then there is Bali, the island of the gods, fragrant with blossom. There are its dances and music too, and even time seems to be magical – this is a country of many mysteries which cannot be fully explained.[2]

The picture which many Japanese draw of the developing countries of the South is that they are hot, poor and dirty. However, in tourist pamphlets, the negative image is erased, and another "South" is presented to the tourists: one of "sun, nature and a South Sea paradise created by the gods."[3] In this tourist geography, the "South" consists of beaches with blue sea and white sand, famous hotels, a culture displayed in famous buildings, food prepared with spices, dazzling ethnic costumes, and exotic dances. In the case of Bali, the phrase "the last paradise," which first appeared in the 1920s, is still used as a tourist slogan today, and Covarrubias' book, *Island of Bali*, is still read as the "bible" of Balinese tourism. The image of paradise as blue sea, white sand, and palm trees continues to be reproduced in the photographs in guidebooks and tourist pamphlets. The photographs of Balinese girls dancing against the backdrop of the temples present the image of the "island of the gods" and the "island of artists." As some pamphlets tell us, "Beautiful beaches, interesting places to see, exotic traditional culture. Colored by the gods and the arts, the paradise of Bali is full of fascination."[4]

2. Hosts and guests

As I discussed in chapter 1, the anthropology of tourism is concerned with what happens in the contact zone between hosts and guests. What happens here in the case of Bali? The tourists come in search of the image of Bali, i.e. "traditional" and "authentic" culture. On the other hand, to the Balinese who receive the tourists, tourism is rated as one part of economic development. It is said that the income from the tourism sector accounts for about 10 percent of the economic activity in the province, though there is no definite information. This being so, traditional culture and economic development are not separate in the case of tourism development in Bali, but must be considered together as a single problem.[5]

However, with the tourists looking for authentic Balinese culture and the Balinese hoping for economic success, the expectations of each group are naturally different. The "hippy problem" was a case in point. From the second half of the 1960s to the first half of the 1970s, Bali was a place where hippies congregated. According to the Balinese, they were an unwelcome presence. Above all, they had a bad reputation for not paying in restaurants, at tourist performances, for woodcarvings, or for staying in hotels. In their peculiar way of thinking, the hippies idealized Bali. They did not think of the Balinese as dancing for economic reasons, but for religious or aesthetic reasons, so they thought there was no need to pay to see the performances (McKean 1973: 235-37). Their idealized image of Bali was in part created by the commercialism of the tourist industry which they disliked, but they failed to recognize this (Tsurumi 1981: 141).

On the relationship between hosts and guests, Philip McKean noted that between the tourists from Sidney and the carvers of Mas village there was generally no shared understanding (McKean 1973: 231). Anette Sanger also pointed out that there was in most cases no verbal communication between the villagers and the tourists (Sanger 1991: 221). At any event, the tourists usually stayed outside of the social world of the Balinese and the social interaction between them was quite limited. In my experience as well, the attitude of the Balinese towards the tourists was often marked by a tendency to ignore them.[6] The Balinese do not stop the tourists from "participating" in their festivals, as long as they are dressed properly, and do not cause trouble. They carry on largely as if the tourists were not there, and if they become deeply involved in the rituals, they often forget about the tourists. While traditional culture has been a focus for tourism in Bali, the reason why it has not broken down is probably the Balinese talent for ignoring the tourists. It is apparent that in the tourist contact zone, direct relations between the hosts and guests are not very frequent. Rather than contacts occurring spontaneously, they occur within a system set up by the tourist industry or the state government.

3. Staging paradise

Dean MacCannell, invoking the social theory of Irving Goffman, looks at tourism from a theatrical point of view. As noted in chapter 2, he sees tourism as the search for authenticity, and suggests that this authenticity may be staged. In our daily lives, cosmetic devices are used to make things look more realistic (rather than real), such as ham with added coloring or breasts enlarged with silicon. This has become an increasingly important trend in tourism. Seafood restaurants decorated with fishing nets, restaurants where the kitchens are visible, the one-day "Apollo experience" at Cape Kennedy in America – all these are examples of "staged authenticity" (MacCannell 1973). The result of this staging in tourism is the creation of a culture that we can call "touristic culture." In the following sections, let us look at some examples of this in relation to tourism in Bali.

Figure 6.1 Entrance to the tourist section of Nusa Dua.

(a) Accommodation

In Bali there are various types of accommodation ranging from high class to low. In tourist areas such as Sanur, Kuta, and Nusa Dua, many high-class resort hotels have been constructed. Elements of Balinese construction methods have been used in the shapes of these buildings and the style of their ventilated ceilings as part of the presentation of "Paradise Bali." A tourist pamphlet runs as follows:

> Mountains and sea, plants, animals, and people. Everything is infused with gods and spirits in Bali, the mysterious island. Its unique culture and natural abundance provide the people who visit it with time to refresh their spirits. . . The peaceful blue ocean, excellent for marine sports. Wide beaches. Banyan trees where the gods live. The natural beauty, which reminds you of the blessings of the gods, and the design of the holiday village, which draws extensively on Bali's culture, harmonize with each other and create a space for mystery and peace.[7]

In the theater at the holiday village people enjoy performances of the *barong* and *kecak* dances, and demonstrations of weaving can also be seen. As Boorstin describes, tourists experience Turkey in the Istanbul Hilton which

Figure 6.2 "Home stay" signboard.

is only an imitation of Turkish style, despite the fact that the real Turkey lies all around it (Boorstin 1963: chap. 3). In the same way, the tourists in Bali experience the island through the microcosm staged in the hotel. This is "showroom Bali" where you can experience the resort ambiance without even stepping outside the hotel. As another guidebook comments: "It is aimed at people who want to remember their honeymoon journey, and people with lots of money who go to 'do the tropics.' Here, Bali is a showroom, but this is not the real Bali."[8]

The real Bali lies not in a "front region" in which social relations are controlled, but in a "back region" where intimate human relationships are prominent. MacCannell has suggested that authenticity is staged within a tourist context in which there are a number of distinct levels of front region and back region (MacCannell 1973: 598), and in Bali a number of different types of settings have been produced, such as "cottages" and "bungalows" which are closer to the back region than a hotel. The blurb in one guidebook talks about the "impression of living in a Balinese house":

Sixty bungalows, laid out in a typical Bali pattern, faithfully reproduce the traditional Balinese house, from the raw materials to the method of construction. The second story is completely made out of bamboo, giving the feeling of freedom that you experience in a Balinese house, and you can look forward to a re-creation of the simple life, far from the noise

Figure 6.3. Cremation procession.

of the city. [...] There is an air conditioner in every room, but when you open the window, a natural breeze blows through the bamboo wall and ceiling, and this is an excellent room for people who dislike air conditioning. Placed near the entrance are an antique style bamboo chair and a stone figure, and the flowers in the garden give the appearance of an ordinary Balinese house. The simplicity, which gives a different feeling from hotels, is an added advantage.[9]

Stepping further into the back region, there are the small establishments called "home stays." In the Ubud region in the interior, part of a royal mansion (*puri*) is often used for home stays. The *puri* consists of several buildings, but the owner makes them available to tourists, with the exception of the main building called the *gudong*. They can stay in a very family-like atmosphere. Sometimes the owner gives lessons in gamelan music and dancing, and sometimes the guests go out with him on fieldtrips to rituals. This kind of tourism is close to "participant observation" in anthropology, and gives a feeling of "living in Bali."

(b) Clothing

As I have already mentioned, tourist guides are obliged to wear traditional Balinese clothing while carrying out their professional duties. In addition,

Figure 6.4 Tourists at a cremation wearing Balinese-style dress.

the tourists are not allowed to wear shorts in Hindu temples, but they must wear a sarong around their waist. One guidebook encourages tourists to "become villagers," and tells them to dress properly in a sarong, especially while participating in temple rituals and village meetings. It provides very precise instructions about clothing on these occasions. For instance, men should wrap a sarong or cloth round their waist, a *saput* or *kampuh* over the top of this, together with a shirt (T-shirts and vests are not allowed), and a headscarf. Women should wear a sarong with a *kebaya* and *selendang* (sash) (Santosa 1988: 18).

As a result, the tourists in Bali can often be seen visiting the temples and walking around wearing batik sarongs. In reality they do not become villagers, but they can at least give an impression of Balinese style by wearing Balinese clothes. By doing so, they stop being onlookers, and become performers themselves. One tourist pamphlet aimed at women issues the following invitation: "Wrap a beautiful colored batik around you, and go really ethnic."[10]

(c) Food

In Balinese tourism the local food is not necessarily stressed. Balinese dishes such as *babi guling* (barbecued pork), *sate* (pork or chicken grilled on a stick) or *lawar* (the Balinese ritual dish of chopped pork dressed with blood) probably add local color. But the dishes mentioned in the tourist pamphlets, such as *nasi goreng* (fried rice), or *mie goreng* (fried noodles) are Indonesian or Indonesian versions of Chinese dishes rather than Balinese, while "lobster dinners" have absolutely no connection with traditional Balinese cuisine. The food served to tourists in Bali is, rather, international. It includes European, Chinese, Indonesian, Japanese, and even Thai and Mexican cuisine. As far as the "internationalization of food" is concerned, nothing beats the big cities in Japan or the U.S. According to one tourist guidebook,

> In the evening in Kuta, there is a great rush to the discos and the bars. If you go a little way down the main street, there is a line of carts with Southeast Asian style food. Passing those, you come and see the places which the average tourist does not get to. The stores and houses are chaotic, and the atmosphere is a mix of nationalities, but this is the flavor of Kuta.[11]

While the internationalization of the food in the tourist areas of Bali is proceeding, it is also important to add that in places like Denpasar, the provincial capital, shops selling Balinese food can also be seen. Generally, these are more frequented by the Balinese than the tourists, and Balinese food is even developing as a takeout food business.

4. Performing arts in the context of tourism

The performing arts are a major attraction in Balinese cultural tourism. The *kecak* and *barong* dances, or the *legong* dance and *Ramayana* ballet are performed for tourists. Their traditional and sacred nature is often stressed as being the essence of Balinese culture. However, as was seen in chapter 3, the important thing is that these performances originated in the encounter between Bali and the West and were created for tourist performance. The stress on the distinction between sacred and secular performances is also recent, as is discussed later. I have already talked about the origins of the *kecak* and *barong* dances in chapter 3, and so here I take up the *legong* dance and *Ramayana* ballet as examples of performances created with the context of tourism in the postwar period (see plate 6.5).

It is said that the *legong* dance can be traced back to performances at the Balinese royal court. It begins with a dance performed by women called *pendet*, which was originally danced in the temples at the times when presentations of flowers and other offerings were made to the gods. During the 1950s, this dance was performed at a reception to welcome President Sukarno

Figure 6.5 *Legong* dance.

and other visitors from the central government, and soon after it was being danced for tourists at places like the Bali Hotel. In reaction to this develop-ment, the Balinese religious officials criticized performances of *pendet* for tourists, on the grounds that it was for divine rather than human entertain-ment. Dances for tourists called *panyembrama* and *tari selamat datang* were therefore devised in the 1960s at KOKAR, the National High School for the Performing Arts founded in 1961 in Denpasar. These dances continue to be used to at tourist receptions at the present day.[12]

The key problem here is that of distinction between sacred and secular performances, or between ritual performances for presentation in places like temples, and performances for tourists. As mentioned in chapter 4, a seminar on sacred and secular dancing was held in 1971 to consider this subject, and the result is that today performances in Bali are divided into three distinct categories. (i) *Wali*: hese are performed in the innermost parts of the temple, and are sacred in nature, for use in ritual. They include dances such as *pendet*, *rejang, baris gede*, and *sanghyang dedari*. (ii) *Bebali*: these are performed in the central part of the temple on the occasion of festivals. They are per-formed in honor of the gods, but they are also intended for pleasure. They include dances such as *wayang, topeng*, and *gambuh*. (iii) *Bali-balihan*: hese are dances for performances near the outermost gate of the temple, and are entirely for entertainment (Yoshida 1992: 162-66).

However, the distinction between *seni sakral* (sacred performance) and *seni provan* (secular or profane performance) is itself expressed in Indone-

Figure 6.6. Tourists watching the *barong* dance.

sian, as it does not exist in Balinese, and is moreover borrowed from European languages. Picard quotes the observations of de Kleen, dating from 1921, in the first article on Balinese dance: "[A]t their temple feasts they combine two good purposes, namely to please their gods and amuse themselves. I would even say that these two things are identical with the Balinese" (Picard 1996: 136). This implies that the sacred/secular performance distinction dates from later, and appears to have come about particularly as a reaction to the development of tourism in Bali. What is also interesting is the fact that the tourist dances are today being presented as part of temple rituals (Picard 1990: 72-73). This means that the performances created for tourist use are apparently having a feedback effect on the Balinese themselves. It also demonstrates, at the same time, that the distinction between "sacred/ ritual" and "secular/tourist" did not exist within the categories of Balinese culture itself.

The *Ramayana* ballet was stimulated by Western ballet, and was created in 1961 at the suggestion of the then minister of communications and tourism for the benefit of tourist audiences at Yogyakarta. This provided a stimulus for Bali as well, and the Balinese version of the *Ramayana* ballet was devised in 1962 for the first anniversary of KOKAR, the national high school for the performing arts mentioned previously. A single spectacle was created by combining Balinese dance with the *Ramayana* story for performance to tourists, and today it is one of the most important Balinese presentations. This kind of devised performance is classed as *sendratari* or "artistic dance

Figure 6.7. *Topeng* dance mask.

drama."[13] New dances created as graduation pieces at the arts school, such as the "rabbit dance" and the "deer dance," are also performed for tourists.

Interestingly, the Balinese themselves are enthusiastic about events like the Bali Arts Festival in which there are contests for newly composed *sendratari* (Picard 1996: 168). Here again, performing arts created for the tourists are by no means for their benefit alone: the Balinese are also adopting them for themselves. As Edward Bruner points out, "If a Balinese troupe performs a dance drama in a temple, we call it religion; if in a concert hall in London, we call it art; if in a beach hotel, we call it tourism. But the distinctions between religion, art and tourism are western categories, not Balinese realities" (Bruner 1995: 238). From the Balinese point of view, these kinds of categories are not mutually exclusive. A Balinese dancer once told me, "a dance is the same everywhere, whether it is in a village, a hotel or a theatre."

Among the tourists today are people learning about music and dancing from the Balinese. Some of them are able to perform well, even by Balinese standards. Sanger mentions an American group which performed at the 1985 Bali Arts Festival and which made a deep impression on the Balinese audience. The ironic thing here, she says, was that the roles of tourists and performers were reversed (Sanger 1991). In Japan as well, the Yamashiro-gumi, a Japanese performance group, have organized "dance tours" since the 1970s, and during my research, Japanese tourists coming to learn Balinese dance were not unusual. Balinese dance does not necessarily have to be performed by Balinese. Moreover, Bandem and deBoer have pointed out the similarity between the dancing in the *calonarang* ritual drama, on which the *barong* dance was based, and the dancers with deranged hair at the disco in Sanur (Bandem and deBoer 1981: 150-51). Contemporary disco and traditional Balinese performance may in this way actually have some common features.

5. The commercialization of performing arts

Now let turn to the groups of performers. Performances in Bali are basically organized by associations called *seka* (or *sekehe*). This is the name for the various types of voluntary associations in Bali, including irrigation associations, and youth associations. Associations for performance are another type, and there are over five thousand of them in Bali as a whole. In 1994, I carried out research on some of these organizations, including groups of performers in Peliatan, Ubud, and Batubulan in Gianyar regency. Performances are mounted for tourists in these areas on a daily basis. What is happening to these groups within this context?

To take Peliatan village as an example, in the village there are now seven *seka* putting on tourist performances, with names like Gunung Sari, Tirta Sari, Gunung Jati, Semar Jati, Semara Madya, and Mekar Sari. These groups are usually based in the sub-units of the village called *banjar*, but their membership is increasingly recruited from beyond the *banjar*. The oldest of them is Gunung Sari, which had the experience of performing at the Colonial Exhibition at Paris in 1931. After the war, in the 1950s, it performed in America. The former leader of the group, a performer at the Paris Exhibition, was a man called Gunka Mandera who died in 1987. He was naturally a major presence in village performances. Currently one of his sons is the leader of Gunung Sari, and another son is the leader of Tirta Sari. Mekar Sari is a women's group and Gunka was their director as well. Semara Madya, a group organized in Banjar Tengah, specializes in the *kecak*. Gunung Jati and Semar Jati, groups from Tegas, another customary village, were organized from two *banjar*, Tegas Kawan and Yangloni.

The membership of the *seka* in 1994 ranged from twenty-five in Gunung Jati to three hundred in Semara Madya. The reason for the size of Semara Madya, in addition to its organization around a *banjar*, is related to the fact that it specializes in the *kecak*, which requires many people. Generally the groups consist of between fifty and one hundred people. The members are mainly divided into musicians and dancers. In addition, the officials include a spokesman, accountant, secretary, and directors of music and dancing. They hold regular meetings once or twice a month, at which financial reports are

83

presented and a variety of policy decisions are taken. The basic job of the *seka* in the village community is to put on performances at the village temple during festivals, what might be called their socio-religious function. There are various other events in addition to this. The Peliatan and Ubud groups also put on other performances on a commercial basis, i.e. for the tourists, perhaps once a week or at no fixed time. The venues include the *banjar* meeting place (*bale banjar*), the courtyards in front of the palace and the temples, and other buildings set up for the purpose. They also make short trips to hotels at Sanur and Nusa Dua to perform, and are invited to perform overseas, for example in Europe, the U.S., and Japan. Many of the groups in Peliatan and Ubud have had the experience of performing overseas.

Mounting performances for tourists is certainly done on a commercial basis. The groups generally get money from ticket sales. However, not all of the income goes to them. The other expenses include payments for tax (which incidentally stood at 20 percent during my research in 1995), security, and for the ticket offices and travel agents handling the tickets. Payments to travel agents account for 50 percent. Thus if 5,000 rupiah of tickets are sold, 1,000 rupiah goes in tax, and 2,500 rupiah in payments to the travel agents who provide the audience. This is in addition to performance expenses including the purchase and maintenance of musical instruments and costumes. When these expenses are deducted, the remainder goes to the *seka*. The way in which it is used and divided up varies from group to group. Some *seka* divide up the money on the basis of each performance. Some groups issue financial statements at their monthly meetings, divide up the money, and carry forward the remainder as savings. Other groups draw up a balance sheet on the day of the *Galungan* festival and, if there is a surplus, they divide it up. But at any rate, when a *seka* has many members each person's share is naturally smaller. Instead of being divided, this money may be used for the development of the *banjar* as a whole. Whatever method is used, this money is not enough to live on, though it does cover incidental expenses. This is the extent of commercialization in Peliatan and Ubud. The groups at Batubulan and Denpasar attract many more tourists than Peliatan and Ubud, and the operations are more like that of a company. Here the musicians and dancers are hired on contract, and a member receives between 75,000 and 100,000 rupiah a month. Some of the members are villagers, and others are students from the performing arts schools working part time. The tourists travel on a bus chartered by the travel agents from the hotels at places like Kuta, and Nusa Dua, and they enjoy performances which last only an hour.

With the commercialization of performances, the issue arises of whether the "sacred" will become commercialized through the performance of sacred works for tourists. The danger that performances will become mannered and standards will drop has also been pointed out. I have already discussed the first of these problems in the previous section. Regarding the second, the Cultural Affairs Office of the provincial government is regulating the situation. As mentioned in chapter 4, groups that want to hold scheduled performances for tourists have to obtain a permit. If groups want to go overseas to perform, the approval of a team of judges is also required. This has given rise to the following practices. In order to get through this inspection, some *seka* invite famous dancers or teachers at the arts school to become their advisors. The result is that the performances have become more standardized, while the school performances have changed the performance traditions in the villages. The impact of standardization and change on performance has probably been greater than that of commercialization through the development of tourism.

6. Touristic culture as self-expression

To summarize, with the introduction of mass tourism into Bali from the start of the 1970s, many of the Balinese officials began to worry about "cultural pollution." Thirty years later, cultural tourism had developed so successfully, that the officials were talking of Bali's "cultural renaissance" (Picard 1996: 165). The "culture" being promoted here, as we have seen in chapter 4, is culture in the form of "art" and especially the performing arts. In Bali today, this cultural production is best represented at the Bali Arts Festival, where there are contests for various arts and crafts – ranging from making *pengjol* (bamboo festival decorations) to cooking, and from *gong kebyar* to Balinese pop art. As for performances, many groups perform *sendratari* and the best group is chosen. But this form of culture, as we saw before, is something newly created since the 1970s, based on the assumption of tourists.

Using this kind of example, Picard suggests that there is a shift from "cultural tourism" to "touristic culture." What he means is that in cultural tourism the main attractions of Balinese culture are being created in response to tourism, and that tourism is becoming the agent of cultural production. So instead of tourism making use of culture in the form of "cultural tourism," we have a situation in which tourism creates what might be called "touristic culture." Rather than seeing culture as a form of "heritage" to be protected, it is seen as a form of "capital," which yields a profit (Picard 1995: 55). Even if this is so, it is not the case that Bali is subordinate to the tourist industry. What the Balinese are actually doing is asserting themselves using tourism. So it might be concluded that touristic culture is a way in which the Balinese people can express themselves, with the tourists as their audience.

Notes

1. *I'll: JAL Ajia (I'll:* Japan Air Lines), April 1992-March 1993 edition. The titles of tourist pamphlets and guidebooks in Japan are often printed in a mixture of Japanese and English language and script.
2. *Look JTB Ajia* (Look, Japan Travel Bureau Asia), April 1990-March 1991 edition.
3. *JTB Pocket Guide: Bali, Indonesia,* 1992 edition.
4. Jet Tour pamphlet for Bali, Lombok and Solo, 1992 edition.
5. The link between culture and the economy in Bali is not new, and artistic performances were traditionally paid for. Sanger (1991: 222) has noted that the villagers did not suddenly become keen capitalists with the arrival of the tourists. The types of performances aimed at the tourists are not much different from traditional ones.
6. On this point, the attitude of the Balinese to the anthropologist arriving in the field is similar, as Geertz has written: "the villagers dealt with us as Balinese seem always to deal with people not part of their life who yet press themselves upon them: as though we were not there. For them, and to a degree for ourselves, we were nonpersons, specters, invisible men" (Geertz 1973: 412).
7. *Club Med: Cheratin Biichi, Shingapôru, Pukketoto, Baritô* (Club Med: Cerating Beach, Singapore, Phuket Island, Bali Island), August 1990-April 1991 edition.
8. *Takurajima Sûpaagaido Ajia: Baritô/Super Guide of Asia: Bali City and Resort,* 1990 edition.
9. *Kadokawa Toraberu Handobukku Balitô/Kadokawa Travel Handbook 11. Bali,* 1988 edition.
10. *Daiyamondo Tsûa: Baritô* (Diamond Tours: Bali Island), October 1990-September 1991 edition.
11. *Takurajima Sûpaagaido Ajia: Baritô/Super Guide of Asia: Bali, City and Resort,* 1990 edition.
12. KOKAR, an abbreviation of Konservatori Karawitan, catered to high school level students. It was reformed and reorganized into Sekolah Menegah Karawitan Indonesia (SMKI). The higher level Arts University, Akademi Seni Tari Indones (ASTI), founded in 1967, was reorganized into Sekolah Tenggi Seni Indonesia (STSI) in 1989.
13. An abbreviation of *seni drama tari,* derived from *seni* (art), "drama," and *tari* (dance).

Chapter 7

Japanese and Balinese Tourism:

Brides Heading for the Island of the Gods

In 1994, when I carried out field research, 1,032,476 foreign tourists visited Bali, of which 211,100 were Japanese. This was the largest number of tourists from any country.[1] In other words, Balinese tourism today cannot be discussed without considering the tourists from Japan. In this chapter, I investigate the significance of tourism in present day Bali focusing on the Japanese tourists, and I pay particular attention to the Japanese women tourists who have gone as far as marrying Balinese men.

1. Japanese images of Balinese tourism

In the present-day tourist industry, Bali is marketed as an Asian beach resort, though, as many travel agents stress, it has a lot more to offer in terms of cultural tourism, as "the island of the gods" or "the island of the arts." This stress on gods and the arts is probably linked to the Western Orientalist image of "the mysterious East," but to the Japanese tourists, who are fellow Asians, this "mysterious East" does not necessarily seem exotic. Matsuda Misa has therefore analyzed Japanese tourism in Bali not only from the perspective of exoticism, but also of nostalgia (Matsuda 1989). To Westerners, Balinese culture with its *barong* dance, Hindu temples, and rice terraces may look exotic, but to the Japanese the *barong* dance is reminiscent of the Japanese lion dance, Hindu temples share features with those in Kyoto and Nara, and rice terraces are quite normal in the rural areas of Japan. However, what Bali probably does do is remind the Japanese of landscapes which have vanished as a result of Japan's rapid urbanization. This nostalgia, as I will discuss later, is an important factor for the Japanese tourists who are attracted to Bali.

One of the most distinctive features of recent Japanese tourist brochures is that they are overflowing with information on what might be called "hotel tourism." These brochures are concerned not with the question whether or not to visit Bali, but rather that of which hotel to stay in. The choice of hotel is becoming the primary means of expressing social differentiation, as discussed by Bourdieu (1984). As we saw in the previous chapters, all the hotels present "Balinese style," and the Bali that is consumed by many Japanese tourists is the one offered by the hotels.

Another feature of Japanese overseas tourist brochures is that the models posing as tourists are non-Japanese, usually with white skin and blond hair. The reason for this is that the tour is "overseas." In these brochures, domestic and overseas tourism are distinguished from each other in ways that range from the language of the advertising copy to the photographs selected for use and the printing font. For domestic tourism, the use of the Japanese *hiragana* script is preferred, and the font looks like Japanese brush calligraphy. As for the photos, subjects are chosen which stress Japanese atmosphere, in order to present a Japanese image. In the case of overseas tourism, in contrast, they select foreign words, *katakana* script, the Roman alphabet, and European and white-skinned models to present an image of being "abroad," which the tourists equate with the models. The Japanese overseas tourists, then, have an ambiguous identity. While abroad, they are forced to play the role of "Westerners," but as I have already shown, in the tours to Bali they are Asian, like the Balinese. So Japanese visitors to Bali oscillate between the three types of identity: Japanese, "Western," and "Asian."

2. Japanese tourists in Bali

Overseas travel for most Japanese used to be an almost inaccessible dream, and the freedom to travel abroad dates only from 1964. In that year, the number of Japanese traveling overseas was 130,000. By 1994, thirty years later, it was over 13,500,000, rising to 16,800,000 in 1997 (Table 7.1). In 1983, leisure and relaxation replaced housing as the main lifestyle objectives of the Japanese (Table 7.2). In parallel with this, the 1980s saw a sudden rise in overseas travel, supported by the high value of the yen.

Within this trend, the number of Japanese visitors to Bali rose sharply at the start of the 1990s, and present-day tourism in Bali cannot be discussed without taking Japanese tourists into account.

Table 7.1. Changing numbers of Japanese overseas tourists.

Year	Number ('000s)	Year	Number ('000s)
1964	128	1981	4,006
1965	159	1982	4,086
1966	212	1983	4,232
1967	268	1984	4,659
1968	344	1985	4,948
1969	493	1986	5,516
1970	663	1987	6,829
1971	961	1988	8,427
1972	1,392	1989	9,663
1973	2,289	1990	10,997
1974	2,236	1991	10,634
1975	2,446	1992	11,791
1976	2,853	1993	11,934
1977	3,151	1994	13,579
1978	3,525	1995	15,298
1979	4,038	1996	16,995
1980	3,909	1997	16,803

Source: Sôrifu , 1998. Tourism Division of the Transport Ministry, based on data from the Ministry of Justice.

What, then, are the distinctive features of Japanese tourism? Let us compare these with the West on the basis of information from the Balinese guides familiar with both Japanese and Western tourists. First, there are differences in the length of stay and ideas about vacations. For Westerners, stays of one or two weeks are normal, compared with between four and six days for Japanese. The typical Japanese schedule is as follows. After arriving on the island in the late afternoon or evening and staying the first night, the first full day includes sightseeing in the town and the *barong* dance. Next they go to the craft villages of Celuk and Mas, or the artists' village of Ubud. In the evening they watch the *kecak* and have a lobster dinner (both fairly popular tour options). Early on the morning of the third day they may fly to Yogyakarta on Java to see the temple at Borobudur, returning the same day. The fourth day involves going slightly further afield, to the Kintamani plateau, or to see temples such as Besakih and Tanah Lot. On the fifth day they are free to go where they like, including souvenir shops, and they return to Japan on a night flight.

Table 7.2. Changing Japanese patterns of expenditure on lifestyles (%).

Year	Clothing	Durables	Food	Leisure	Housing
1973.1	1.9	7.0	14.4	20.2	30.5
1974.1	2.4	6.8	24.5	13.8	26.7
1974.11	2.6	6.8	24.1	14.7	25.1
1975.5	2.4	6.7	21.9	16.0	27.9
1975.5	3.1	5.8	20.7	16.5	28.0
1976.5	2.3	5.7	19.5	18.1	29.4
1976.11	2.4	6.3	20.3	16.0	29.5
1977.5	1.8	5.2	21.8	18.1	25.3
1978.5	2.6	5.2	16.3	21.5	30.3
1979.5	2.5	6.2	15.2	23.5	30.0
1980.5	2.2	7.4	17.3	19.9	28.1
1981.5	2.1	6.0	17.2	22.6	27.1
1982.5	2.0	6.8	16.3	21.2	25.7
1983.5	2.1	5.1	14.5	26.3	25.2
1984.5	2.0	5.6	15.1	27.6	25.7
1985.5	1.8	4.8	14.5	27.6	25.0
1986.5	1.7	4.6	13.2	29.0	26.4
1987.5	2.1	4.6	15.1	31.6	24.1
1988.5	1.5	4.4	13.4	31.7	24.1
1989.5	1.4	4.0	15.0	33.7	23.1
1990.5	1.6	4.1	12.6	37.2	22.6
1991.5	1.5	4.1	11.0	37.1	23.1
1992.5	1.3	3.5	13.0	37.0	25.8
1993.5	1.1	3.7	13.2	37.1	25.8
1994.5	1.2	4.0	13.6	35.3	24.8
1995.5	1.3	4.4	15.4	35.3	25.1
1996.5	1.3	3.8	15.5	36.6	25.0
1997.5	1.7	3.1	16.3	36.2	25.1

Source: Sôrifu 1998, based on "Kokumin seikatsu ni kansuru seiron chôsa" [Survey of Japanese lifestyles], May 1997. "Durables" includes vehicles, electrical goods and furniture.

Western tourists, in contrast, usually do nothing on the first and second day after their arrival. They begin the optional tours that interest them from the third day. They also lie out by the pool and enjoy their vacation, doing

Figure 7.1. Japanese tour group.

nothing (the root meaning of "vacation" being "empty"). The Japanese, on the other hand, are busy seeing the sights. When the Japanese make their hotel reservations, they generally specify that it must be a room facing the sea, but, as the Balinese guides note cynically, they may not have any time to look at it, because they are out of the hotel from the early morning until late in the evening.

The Japanese pattern of tourism involves a short but busy stay, and this is reinforced by the fact that many Japanese use package tours offered by the travel industry, which provide a fixed number of days in Bali. This packaging of tourism has reduced the costs of travel, but the content of the tour has also increasingly followed a set pattern. Many Western tourists, in contrast, plan their own trip. Another difference is that Bali is closer to Japan so that there are a large number of people making repeat trips. The Western tourists, however, try to experience it to the full as a once-in-a-lifetime trip, because of the distance. Furthermore, as the guides observe, Western tourists go to "listen," while Japanese tourists go to "see."[2] In other words, when they go to the tourist spots, Westerners ask many questions, and they listen carefully until they understand. The Japanese generally do not ask questions, and as soon as they have had a quick look, they are finished.

In terms of shopping, the Japanese buy souvenirs not only to remember their travels, but also because of social obligations. The amount they buy may therefore be considerable. The Japanese make up about 20 percent of the foreign tourists in Bali, but they are said to account for 50 percent of the money spent on souvenirs. Even though they do not buy as much as they do in Hawaii, Singapore or Hong Kong, they still look out for brand name goods in Bali as well. The proportion of the tour that the Japanese devote to shopping is very large compared with people from the West.

In the Japanese language of tourism, as Brian Moeran's analysis suggests, ideas such as "making yourself at home," "being at ease," and "doing things your own way" are stressed (things which are, in fact, normally prevented in Japanese society) (Moeran 1983). In reality, however, tourism for the Japanese is itself a kind of work, with everybody buying souvenirs, taking photographs, and feeling unhappy if they leave anything out. On photographs, Susan Sontag writes as follows:

> Most tourists feel compelled to put the camera between themselves and whatever is remarkable that they encounter. Unsure of other responses, they take a picture. This gives shape to experience: stop, take a photograph, and move on. The method especially appeals to people handicapped by a ruthless work ethic – Germans, Japanese, and Americans. Using a camera appeases the anxiety which the work-driven feel about not working when they are on vacation and supposed to be having fun. They have something to do that is like a friendly imitation of work: they can take pictures. (Sontag 1979: 10)

According to some of the Balinese guides, the Japanese pretend to be indifferent when they encounter other Japanese tourists during their stay in Bali. Here the ambiguous identity of the Japanese overseas tourists becomes apparent. As I said before, they are "Westerners" when they travel overseas, and so they must not be addressed as Japanese. There is also the question of territorial ethnicity in tourism. For example, when the Japanese tourists start to arrive, Western tourists leave for the "unspoiled" areas where there are no Japanese. If, therefore, a mass of Japanese start to come to Ubud, Western tourists go to Candidasa in eastern Bali, or sometimes to the island of Lombok, or to eastern Indonesia. Japanese tourists, on the other hand, do not particularly like tourists from Taiwan, and when they are with a Taiwanese group in a restaurant they may claim that they are noisy or untidy. Furthermore, foreign tourists and domestic (i.e. Indonesian) tourists tend to use different classes of hotels and restaurants. So, even though the tourist destination is a place where people of many different nationalities encounter each other, it is also a place where they are segregated as well. This kind of observation is based on stereotypes and there is probably a lot of individual variation.

However, the group-oriented Japan Airlines package tours ("Jalpak") targeted at Japanese tourists underwent a change in the 1990s, with more stress on individual choice and the word *Airu* (I'll). Also, the concepts of life style have changed from *moretsu* (intense, hard) to *byutifuru* (beautiful, soft) with the appearance of the generation known in Japan as *shinjinrui*, the "new kind of people." Even in tourism, busy groups have begun to give way to free individualism.

Amidst these changes, some tourists describe Bali as "the island which touches your heart" with a stress on the word "heart" or "*kokoro*" in Japanese.

Bali has become increasingly popular. People who have experienced the island find their hearts moved, and they come back to visit the island one more time, and then another. We can regain the things we have lost one by one, surrounded by the gods, by nature, and by the wise people who have chosen to live among them. As if in a second homeland, the days pass with our hearts completely at peace.[3]

Here Bali is no longer exotic. It becomes a spiritual homeland for those who visit it repeatedly. A women's magazine once published a special issue on going to Bali in search of "healing." It says:

Both love and work are a struggle. Self-healing is difficult while at the same time fighting. Mobile phones, the departure bells in crowded trains, the electrical noises at pedestrian crossings – if you are tired of everything like this, give it up and leave Japan. Bali is only about ten hours from Narita. There, along with the dazzling blue sky and the scents, people welcome you with warm, smiling faces that are somehow familiar. While the balmy breezes blow, yogurt and the essence of tropical flowers, and the natural beauty treatment provided by the sea will be the best cure for your body. This is your natural reward for your tired body. So if you want to heal yourself, cross the sea.[4]

Bali is here taken as a healing place where young Japanese women can recover from the battlefield of the work places in Japan. The link between "healing" and tourism is not necessarily new in Japan. From the Edo period there was a tradition of hot water cures, with people visiting hot springs to "rest their bones." Even in domestic tourism in Japan today, going to hot springs is still the most popular reason for travel among both men and women (57.4 percent) (Sôrifu 1995: 37). In recent years there has been an *onsen* (hot spring) tourism boom especially among young women, perhaps because young working women need a rest. At any rate, once-in-a-lifetime tourism abroad has changed from busy sightseeing, eating and shopping to finding space for rest and physical recovery.

3. Brides heading for the Island of the Gods

An important feature of Japanese overseas tourism is that nearly 40 percent of the female tourists are young women in their twenties (Figure 7.4).[5] Generally in Japan, it is difficult for women to travel abroad once they get married, and especially once they start looking after children. So it is the carefree singles who are free to travel. As Karen Kelsky points out, they are "the most enthusiastic and committed travelers of any demographic group in the world" (Kelsky 1996: 175). This is the case in Bali as well.

In the context of this active involvement of young Japanese women in Balinese tourism, I want to examine one particular phenomenon, that of Japanese women tourists who marry Balinese men.[6] According to the Japanese consulate in Bali, there were more than 200 of these marriages in 1995, and allowing for some who have not registered their residence, the real number is at least 400. This is a phenomenon of the 1990s.[7] During my research in 1995, I was able to interview 30 Japanese wives in Bali, and will summarize the results in the three following points.

First, many of these women were born around 1960. In other words, they belong to the generation that grew up during the period of high-speed growth in the Japanese economy. During this period, the Japanese archipelago was transformed drastically. Because of this, these women have discovered "the landscapes they had lost" – empty spaces and rough and muddy roads – in Bali, and they think nostalgically of the "old Japan."

Second, an overwhelming number of them come from major metropolitan areas such as Tokyo and Osaka. In other words, the "brides heading for the Island of the Gods" are mainly an urban phenomenon. In addition, they find that they are unable to adapt to urban life in present-day Japan. Dissatisfied with Japan or unable to adapt to it, they feel that they are rediscovering their "real selves" in Bali.

Third, many of them followed a similar pattern: they came to Bali first as tourists, were charmed wherever they went on the island, made repeated visits, and ended up marrying. Here there seemed to be two patterns, typical of Kuta and Ubud respectively. Kuta is a stronghold of surfing, with noisy discos which are crowded in the evenings. Ubud, in contrast, is an arts village in

Table 7.3 Distribution of Japanese overseas tourists by age and sex (%).

Age	Men	Women	Total
0-9	2.5	2.9	2.7
10-19	4.3	6.5	5.3
20-29	18.6	36.8	26.9
30-39	21.6	16.0	19.2
40-49	22.0	11.9	17.4
50-59	18.2	13.8	16.2
60 +	12.8	11.8	12.3

Source: Sôrifu, 1998. Tourism Division of the Transport Ministry, based on figures for 9,134,762 men and 7,667, 988 women.

the interior, where people live surrounded by music and painting. The important point is, however, that the women moved to Bali because of their cultural interests, whether in marine sports or Balinese music and dance.

As for the attraction of marrying Balinese men, they described it as follows:

When I was in Japan I didn't want to get married. I thought that marriage led to trouble. But when I came across the personality of the Balinese, I have changed my mind.

He was affectionate and good-looking. It wasn't that he was Balinese, he was just good.

I like the sea and came to Bali to surf, but I got picked up at a disco. It's the right time to marry I think. . .

In married life here, my husband gives me a lot of help with looking after the children and with work.

The family is huge, and it's really good to want someone and to be wanted.

In this way these women first woke up to the possibility of marriage, having children, and a family when they came to Bali. There is no particularly clear reason as to why it had to be Bali, though their comments do express boredom with living in Japan.

> Aren't people unkind in Japan today? When I asked people the way, they ignored me.

> The faces of the present-day Japanese are expressionless. Looking at them is unpleasant.

> If I am in Japan for about two or three weeks, the energy I bring back from Bali disappears, and I begin to think that I've had enough. Bali is a much cozier place to live.

> Japan is full of gadgets and information, but I always feel they have got things wrong. In Bali there is little information, so you don't get confused. That is a pleasure.

These comments suggest that they are "refugees" from what Karel van Wolferen (1994) describes as the "Japanese system that fails to make people happy." Certainly marriage with a Balinese partner does not necessarily work out well, and there are also many difficulties resulting from differences in customs. However, they generally think that Japan's "prosperity" is not everything, and that it is not necessarily a good place to live.

4. Transnational living

In his book, *Nihonjin o yameru hôhô* (The way to stop the Japanese), the Australian-based Japanese sociologist, Sugimoto Yoshio, says the following:

> Hidden in all the fuss about people taking refuge in Japan is the fact that the problem of people who escape from Japan has completely dropped out of view. Attention is only one-way. The people fleeing from Japan, about whom nobody gives a thought, come from the majority in Japanese society. Most people only shrug their shoulders when the question of why this happens is mentioned. Such is the self-image of the contemporary Japanese. However, if you observe closely the reality of large numbers of Japanese scattered overseas who have lost patience with Japanese

society, you can actually see that people are leaving all over the place. The number of people currently settled overseas is said to be over 700,000, and of these about 10 percent are these kinds of refugees, so the total probably stands at over 70,000. (Sugimoto 1993: 175)

A maximum of four hundred Japanese brides in Bali are only a very small part of this phenomenon, but a similar situation can be found in New York, London and Hong Kong as well. Ieda Shoko in her sensational best seller, *Yellow Cab*, also seems to understand the background to this (Ieda 1991).[8]

In Japan today, the marriage age of women is the highest in the world (26.6 years on average in 1997, according to the welfare ministry). Young Japanese women nowadays often do not seem to find much of a positive reason to get married, and are therefore reluctant to do so. Furthermore, in some villages in contemporary Japan where depopulation continues, the exodus of women to the cities has led to a dearth of women, and it is common knowledge that brides are "imported" from places such as the Philippines and Sri Lanka. But as the Asian brides move into the Japanese villages, the Japanese women who have left for the cities are moving overseas. What is the significance of this flow? And where a wider choice of marriage partners has led to the development of an international "marriage market," how is marriage in Japan rated?

To answer these questions we have to consider the position of women in Japanese society. The places in which women's potential can be fully utilized are quite limited. The promotion prospects of women in the workplace are improving to some extent, but with employment recruitment slowing due to the recent economic recession, the first people to be excluded are women. The feminist sociologist Ueno Chizuko says that when the economic bubble appeared to burst, the principle of women's employment under the equal opportunities legislation became empty lip service only. Certainly on a one-to-one basis, the relationship between men and women is changing, but in enterprises and other organizations, as Ueno points out, things have hardly changed at all over the last 20 or 30 years (Ueno 1996: 315). Women go abroad as tourists, students, or to look for work, not only in Bali but also in Hong Kong, London, and New York. The exodus abroad of Japanese women resulting in international marriages seems to me to be their reaction to a Japanese system that fails to make them happy.

Here are two other examples to compare with the Japanese brides in Bali. One is the study by Suzy Kruhse-Mount Burton of sex tourism among Australian men in Southeast Asia. According to her, Australian men were unable to find women satisfied with "traditional men" in sexual relationships with Australian women, but in their sexual encounters with Thai, Filipina, and Indonesian women from Southeast Asia they were able to find what they wanted. In this case, traditional notions of male identity were related to sex tourism (Kruhse-Mount Burton 1995). A second example is marriage between Japanese men and the *Japayuki-san*, i.e. women from the Philippines coming to Japan. These kinds of marriages numbered over ten thousand a year in the late 1980s. The official at the Japanese embassy in Manila who handled the visa applications of Filipina wives is said to have muttered, "Aren't there any women in Japan?" According to Hisada Megumi, Japanese men unable to find partners in Japan to help them cope with loneliness and isolation were able to find them among women from the Philippines, and the result was marriage (Hisada 1992). I am not defending the Japanese sex industry which is linked to both the flow of foreign women into Japan and sex tourism in Southeast Asia. What I want to draw attention to is that these phenomena provide insights into unresolved problems in traditional gender relations, either within a single country or a single ethnic group.

To get back to Bali, as the number of Japanese women getting married in Bali has increased, Japanese society in Bali, and especially the character of the Japanese Association there, has also changed. The Japanese abroad in many countries often form a very closed group and hardly mix with the local society. However, in the case of Bali, what is remarkable is that the Japanese women who have married Balinese do participate in the Japanese Association, and they are able to play a role in opening it up to Balinese society. This was illustrated by an event, the sixth "Bon Dance" in celebration of the Japanese Buddhist festival held at the Nusa Dua Hilton in September 1994, organized by the Japanese Association in Bali. The interesting thing about it was that, rather than being the usual expression of Japanese communal identity, the Bon Dance expressed the energy of the hybrid community in Bali. The children of mixed parentage danced, while their Balinese fathers took photographs. The Japanese women of the Nyonya-kai (the women's section of the association) performed on *jugog* (bamboo instruments), and danced the *joged bungbung* (a popular Balinese folk dance) to the music.

How will this jumble of different cultures work out in the future? For now, the period of observation is too short to give an answer, but situations where people live in this way are usually discussed today using the concept of "diaspora." This term originally referred to the permanent separation of the Jews from their homeland, and has been extended to transnational migrants in general. Along with the development of globalization, the numbers

Figure 7.2. Birthday celebration for the baby of a Japanese wife.

of diaspora peoples living separated from their areas of origin have greatly increased.

5. Living in-between

In this chapter, I have examined a spectrum of phenomena ranging from tourism to migration, using the case of Japanese tourists in Bali. To the Japanese, Bali is first and foremost a South Seas tourist resort. However, at the same time it has a fascination that goes beyond that of a resort. "Repeaters" come back many times, and brides head for the Island of the Gods.[9] After their marriage, many of the wives work in the tourist sector in places such as souvenir shops, boutiques, restaurants, and "home stay" accommodation. It is interesting that many of them have no idea of giving up their Japanese nationality and becoming Indonesian: they do not want to abandon the country they have migrated from. Instead, perhaps they are the ultimately successful tourists, if we use "tourism" in the same way as MacCannell – as a search for authenticity or our own "real selves" (MacCannell 1976: 13). This phenomenon can be expressed another way. According to these women, whose lives extend over two countries, the difference between traveling and living is not all that great. In one of his articles, James Clifford has speculated about the difference between the two: for the people who spend their lives traveling back and forth between the Caribbean and Brooklyn in New York, the question which has to be asked is not so much "Where are you from?" as "Where are you between?" (Clifford 1992: 109).

This kind of lifestyle cannot be understood using the static equation of ethnic groups with cultures by anthropologists of the past, in which it was assumed that if a particular people existed in a particular area, so did a particular culture. Rather than living "within" their culture, these people live "in between" cultures, making up their own. This is where I think the forms of living which will dominate the twenty-first century are taking shape.

Notes

1. Figures from the Bali state government tourist office. These figures include numbers of people entering the country at Ngurah Rai International Airport, but people who entered the country at other airports in Indonesia are not included. In 2001, the number of foreign visitors to Bali was 1,467,424, which included 363,697 Japanese. These figures showed an increase over those for 1994. By 1997, the number of Australian tourists had overtaken that of the Japanese, probably as a result of the continuing economic recession in Japan.

2. According to the "White Paper on Tourism" (Sôrifu 1995: 43), the main reasons people went abroad included natural scenery (63 percent, ranking first) and historical sites, culture, museums and art galleries (ranking third). It is clear that the main point was to "see" things.

3. *I'll JAL Bali Island*, April-September 1996.

4. *Rinku*, 1996, July-August edition.

5. As for men, according to the 1998 "White Paper on Tourism" (Sôrifu 1998: 38), men in their twenties made up less than 20 percent. No particular age group predominated, and travelers were scattered across the whole age range. The difference between men and women may be one of the reasons for the so-called "Narita Airport Divorce."

6. Strictly speaking, not all the husbands were Balinese, but they included other Indonesians such as Javanese, people from Lombok, Minangkabau, and Chinese.

7. This is a topic that has already been taken up by the mass media. See for instance, "Brides Heading for the Island of the Gods" (Asahi Shinbun, 94.6.19); "The Lives of 200 Japanese Women Who Have Become 'Bali Island wives'" (*Shûkan Shinchô*, 95.9.7); and "Illusions of Paradise" (Aera, 96.6.17). The educational television channel of NHK (Nihon Hôsô

Kyôkai or Japanese Broadcasting Corporation) broadcast a documentary, "Goodbye Japan: Brides Heading for the Island of the Gods" (1996.3.13). The *Shûkan Shinchô* article reported that with the high value of the yen, Japanese women were in search of sex in "paradise Bali." As a result marriages with Balinese men were increasing quickly, but once the Japanese women woke up from their dream of "paradise," their lives in Bali were not necessarily happy. There was a strong local reaction to sensationalist treatment and irresponsible content of the article, and the Japanese Association in Bali protested to the *Shûkan Shinchô* reporter.

8. Numerous other books have been published in addition to this, such as those by Yamamoto Michiko (1993), Shimoju Akiko (1999), and Kida Midori (1998), to mention but a few.

9. In Japan today, many other books are being published on Bali in addition to guidebooks. These go beyond tourism in that they are based on the authors' own experiences in Bali, in addition to literary imagination. It is probably correct to talk about a "Bali phenomenon" in Japanese publishing.

Chapter 8

Alternative Tourism: New Developments

Just as "grand narratives" of development are said to be a thing of the past, various attempts are being made to move beyond modern mass tourism. In Bali, too, there is also a search for new policies as the development of tourism has accelerated. In this chapter I look at new, alternative forms of tourism on the island, with reference to the introduction of village tourism in Penglipuran, Bangli regency.

1. Alternative tourism

As stated in the first chapter, by the 1990s tourism looked set to become a core industry for many countries in the twenty-first century. As a result, experiments in tourism flourished in both the developed and the developing countries in the search for economic benefits. Focusing on Southeast Asia, tourism in Thailand had already overtaken rice as the top earner of foreign exchange by the 1990s. In the Philippines, it ranked second, and in Singapore it ranked third (Hitchcock, King, and Parnwell 1993: 1).

In Indonesia, as we have already seen, from the start of the 1980s the government also decided to invest resources in tourism as a foreign currency earner, rather than in oil. But this "smokeless industry" did not produce results that were entirely clean. Problems arose along with tourism development, such as the breakdown of the natural environment, the unequal distribution of profits, commercialism, and the destruction of local tradition in addition to the spread of drugs and prostitution. These have been strongly denounced (e.g. Matsui 1993). Even in Hawaii tourists have experienced strong antagonism, as reported by George Pfafflin: "We don't want tourism. We don't want you. We don't want to be degraded as servants and dancers. That is cultural prostitution. I don't want to see a single one of you in Hawaii.

There are no innocent tourists" (Pfafflin 1987: 578). As a result, new, alternative forms of tourism are becoming the subject of research.[1] In 1989 in Zakopane in Poland, the theme of the first general meeting of the International Academy for the Study of Tourism was a theoretical overview of these alternative forms (Ishimori 1990; Smith and Eadington 1992). "Sustainability" is becoming the key word in this new direction in development (Yamashita, Din, and Eades 1997: 24-26). In this chapter, I will focus on this new wave of tourist developments and initiatives in Bali, especially "village tourism" which has been growing since the early 1990s.

2. The acceleration of tourist development in Bali

As mentioned before, in 1997 the number of foreign tourists in Bali was over 1.2 million. Tourism had previously been confined to the southern part of Bali (Badung and Gianyar regencies), but now it has spread to all parts of the island, such as Karangasem regency (Candidasa) in the east; Buleleng regency (Lovina) in the north; and Tabanan (Tanah Lot) and Jembrana regencies in the west. In addition, the neighboring islands including Lombok, Flores, and Komodo in eastern Indonesia are being added to the tourist map.

In the project to develop the Nusa Dua region in the 1980s, people were worried about its bad influence on the local residents, and they worked out a means of separating them from the tourists. And so the international hotels became a microcosm in which "paradise Bali" was staged, and a place where the tourists could enjoy their holiday innocuously. This apparently kept them well segregated in a kind of "tourist ghetto" (Maurer 1979: 36), but there is still lingering dissatisfaction among the type of tourists who want to experience a different culture, and therefore want to come into contact with the local people. The Nusa Dua development also produced some resentment on the part of the local people themselves. In short, though the government was buying up sites in order to stimulate employment, the hotels appeared not to be employing local people on the grounds that they did not speak foreign languages, even though it was becoming increasingly obvious that hotels were employing Javanese migrant workers from outside the island. From the hotels' point of view, it would have been difficult to operate if they had employed only Balinese who had a reputation for taking time off for festivals to suit themselves. This seems to have been a situation in which they had to employ Javanese.

Moreover, in recent years there has been an acceleration of commercialization, and this is particularly evident in the rapid rise of land prices in the tourist areas. This is especially true of Legian Avenue, the popular main street in Kuta where prices in the 1990s rose to ten times their former level. At the time of my fieldwork in 1990, the price stood at two million rupiah per square meter (about 150,000 yen or U.S.$1,500 at the then rate of exchange). The reason for the price rise was the influx of outside capital from Jakarta and elsewhere. Also, many of the people running the rows of shops on this street were foreigners, including Japanese. Despite the differences, similar conditions now extend to Ubud in the interior which is becoming a second Kuta. The idea that Bali is slipping out of the hands of the Balinese, was reflected in a song sung at the Indonesian popular music festival in 1987 by the son of the former President Sukarno, the singer Guruh Sukarno Putra, entitled, "Kembakikan Baliku," "Give back my Bali!" (In fact, President Sukarno's mother, Guruh Sukarno's grandmother, came from Bali.)

3. Integrated tourist villages: the frontier of Balinese tourism

The nature of Balinese tourism is changing in a number of ways. Many different forms are developing, with accommodation ranging from cheap lodgings at U.S.$10 a night, to high-class hotels at over U.S.$500 a night; and with special interest tours ranging from backpacking to dancing lessons. At the request of the government tourism office, a research team based at Gadjah Mada University in Yogyakarta carried out research for a tourism master plan for Bali in this new era. The project began with the five-year plan of 1989–94: it looked at Nusa Dua in the 1970s and 1980s as a typical example of mass tourism, and it focused on alternative tourism in an attempt to find a tourist strategy for Bali (Universitas Gadjah Mada 1992: 1). The result was the proposal of a type of tourism based on the *desa wisata terpadu*, or "integrated tourist village." According to the governor of Bali, Ida Bagus Oka, this village proposal was an attempt to develop sustainable tourism in Bali and mark out the direction for tourist development on the island (Oka 1992: 127). The integrated tourist villages are not villages created for tourist use, but ordinary villages which present their culture to tourists in an integrated way. According to the report of the research team, these types of villages are defined as:

> village areas which have an atmosphere reflecting the authenticity of the Balinese village in regards to social and cultural activities, everyday customs, buildings, and the traditional use of space, while at the same time able to provide the infrastructure, attractions, catering, and accommodation required for tourists. (Universitas Gadjah Mada 1992: 1)

Three villages were selected for a pilot project: Jatiluwi in Tabanan regency, Sebatu in Gianyar regency, and Penglipuran in Bangli regency. These three villages have their own local color. Jatiluwi is a village with beautiful rice terraces, so that its tourism focuses on nature and rice cultivation. Sebatu is a craft village famous for woodcarving, with an ancient Hindu temple called Gunung Kawi. Penglipuran preserves the "traditional" village spatial structure in the layout of the houses.

Here I will describe the case of Penglipuran village, which I was able to visit during my research in 1994 and 1995. It is one of the customary villages belonging to the Kubu division of Bangli regency, in the central part of Bali.[2] This region is mountainous, and its agricultural potential is therefore limited. It lies a little off the main road which passes through the town of Bangli, the regency headquarters, and which links the north and southern parts of the island. It is surrounded by forest, bamboo groves, and fields, with the paddy fields located further away. Up to now, these resources have provided the villagers' incomes. The population of the village is about 750, made up of 170 households. Of the working population of around 400, officials, traders, and craftsmen each make up about 10 percent, and the other 70 percent are all farmers. The core of the villagers consists of the 45 households who own the paddy fields. The others make their living as tenant farmers or from other kinds of fields where tree crops such as vanilla, coffee, cloves, cocoa, and lacquer are cultivated.[3]

The reason why this relatively poor village was chosen as a possible "integrated tourist village" was its "traditional" appearance. In the residential part of the village, groups of houses are arranged on both sides of the road running from north to south. Each of the houses is laid out in a long rectangle of about the same size. The frontage is narrow, about five meters, but the house runs back a long way, as much as twenty meters. Each house is furnished with a gate built in the same style, forming the entrance facing on to the central street. At the northeast corner of each plot is the household shrine, and to the west is a kitchen combined with a sleeping room, enclosed by a wall. To the south is a ritual building in the form of a pavilion with no walls, and to the west of this are buildings used for living and sleeping.

In the central area between the houses running from north to south is a building used by the villagers for meetings, and the granary where the rice produced in the paddy fields on publicly owned land is stored. This rice is donated for rituals in the village temple, or it is sold and the money is used for temple administration. On the north side of the village road is the village temple set against the forest, and on the eastern side of this there is another cluster of temples. A number of other temples are spread throughout the

Figure 8.1. Balinese rice terraces.

forest behind. The graveyard and the temples for appeasing the spirits of the dead are located on the outskirts of the village, extending along the road to the south. The village is thus located along the slope of a range of hills. The highest area in the north is the domain of the gods and ancestors, the central part is the area where the villagers themselves live, and the lowest part is the realm of the dead. In its form, therefore, it embodies the Balinese worldview. This principle of arrangement is not limited to Penglipuran, but generally corresponds to other Balinese villages as well, though here it is particularly compact and easy to grasp.

Tourists in Penglipuran therefore walk around the village and experience its traditional layout. If they have the chance, they visit a local house with villagers as guides, interact with the villagers, and hear about their customs. According to Mr. A., a Balinese official working at the government department of tourism in Jakarta, the essence of Balinese culture lies in the villages, so this is where the resources for promoting tourism on the island lie. This strategy is aimed at tourists who are "repeaters" and who want to see "alternative" Bali, rather than the first-time tourists.

Tourists pay an entry fee on entering the village. The sale of entry tickets started in April 1993, and in October 1994 they cost 1,000 rupiah (or about U.S.$0.50). The village youth group manages the ticket system, and they also act as guides around the village. The village has groups performing gamelan music and various types of dances on ritual occasions. Visiting

Figure 8.2. Penglipuran. Tourists and a guide in local dress

Penglipuran at the time of a temple festival is a unique opportunity to learn about the traditional life of the village.

The selling point of the village is "traditional Balinese culture," but it must be emphasized that this is not simply tradition that has been unconsciously transmitted from long ago. It is, rather, something that is being manipulated, recreated and consumed within the contemporary economic, social, and cultural context. The current appearance of Penglipuran is the result of repair work for a planned visit by President Suharto in 1991, though the visit never took place. Mr A., the government tourist department official already mentioned, also explains that, even though tradition is being preserved, the aim is not to keep Balinese villages exactly as they were. The people and their culture are definitely not static, so what is required is "dynamic preservation."

4. Sustainable tourism

Sustainable tourism can be defined as development which will benefit the people of today without harming the resources to be shared by future generations or their prosperity. In other words, it is promotion of development that maintains a balance between ecosystem, society and culture. According to Emanuel de Kadt, the development of sustainable tourism involves the following features: protection of the environment; small-scale production; recognition of essentials beyond material consumption; recognition of the necessity to take future generations into account as well; and decision making from the bottom up (de Kadt 1992: 50). In this form of development, the most important points for the societies in each region are the process of decision making in development planning, and participation in planning so as to have an impact on its implementation.

In order to meet the demand for mass tourism in Bali, resort developments which remodeled nature on a grand scale took place at the instigation of government and business, such as Nusa Dua in the 1980s. Today, however, the tourist market in Bali has become almost saturated in relation to the size of the island and its population. The diversification of tourism, and the increasing number of repeaters, means that more flexible alternative forms of tourism are needed, and it was in response to this that village tourism was introduced. On the other hand, the Kubu division of Bangli, to which Penglipuran belongs, is classified as *desa tertinggal*, that is to say, "the most backward" in terms of village development. For this reason, the Bangli regency government plans to place the district in the forefront of present-day development by turning Penglipuran into an integrated tourist village. In this way the out-migration of the younger people to the cities would be stopped by strengthening their links with the village, while at the same time conserving traditional Bali. This means that tourism in Penglipuran is an exercise in village renewal, which will allow adaptation to this new period of development.[4] Against this background, the construction of the facilities necessary for the integrated tourist village has proceeded with the help of the Bali state government, including a meeting place (*bale banjar*) in 1992–93, a "model room" open to tourists in 1993–94, and a car park in 1994–95. In addition, the forest and bamboo grove behind the temple to the north have been maintained as a center for traditional Balinese bamboo craft production. There is a plan to promote the use of this in tourism as well.

From the viewpoint of sustainable tourist development, this case is interesting in another way. Even though it is a development project which has been carried out under government leadership, it involves the local people. The entry tickets for the village and the car park are an important source of income, 60 percent of which goes to Bangli regency, and 40 percent to Penglipuran. The income from the tickets in August and September 1994 amounted to 1,063,000 rupiah – about U.S.$500. This is a small amount, but it is a source of income, and if the income from tourism continues to rise steadily, it will be significant for the village.

However, I have to point out that the meeting place and model room at Penglipuran seem to be of little practical use. Even though they have opened up the "traditional village" and turned into a tourist place, the villagers themselves have been confused about what to do with it. When I visited the village head of Penglipuran, it was he who asked me my opinion on how to develop tourism in the village and whether I had any good ideas. Five members of the village youth group also received six weeks of training, studying tourism at the tourist development center at Nusa Dua.

As for the tourists, they were certainly interested in the lives of the villagers, but did not seem to enjoy touring the village very much because they did not speak the language, and also because they were not certain how far they could intrude in the lives of the villagers. It seemed that travel agents and contract guides also provide information on the villages, but how far a guide who comes from elsewhere can enter into the world of the village is a question. Anyway, this new type of tourism has come into being and, as with ecotourism, it probably requires the development of tourists with a new kind of awareness, as well as a new system of providing guides who are qualified as cultural instructors.

5. Development and identity

Village tourism in Bali is only just starting up, and as yet it is not possible to say whether it has been a success. When I visited Penglipuran village for the first time, I asked a girl playing in front of her house for directions. The girl who was about ten years old was so nervous talking to a foreigner that she stood rigidly to attention and could hardly utter a word. I was surprised since I had not seen this kind of reaction to outsiders among Balinese children for a while. It will be interesting to see how this naive girl develops in the future along with tourism in her village, though a little more time is still necessary. An evaluation of the effects of sustainable development cannot be carried out over a short period. At any rate, things are not so clear-cut that the influence of the development of tourism on the local society can be seen as either "good" or "bad." As I have suggested by looking at the example of Bali, there are certainly some elements of "traditional culture" that fit with tourism. Tourism also stimulates traditional culture, and this may result in the creation of new culture. In addition, tourism heightens the self-awareness of the local people in tourist areas, and strengthens their identity. This tendency of the local people to look inwards is certainly a process of major importance, both in the developed and developing countries, in addition to the process of development itself.

What should also be noted is that the identity of local people in a tourist area is constructed on the basis of a delicate balance in a process of bargaining with the outside world. I have already stressed on several occasions that the way of life, the way of thinking, and the values of people rooted in the area have to be respected in the process of development. But as Okamoto correctly suggests, people at present are experiencing the problems of being unable to compete if they have access to only local knowledge gained from living in a particular area (Okamoto 1996: 169-77). This suggests that returning to a way of life rooted in a particular region is probably impossible. The problem ultimately is, therefore how the people handle the process of accommodation to the dynamics of the macro system surrounding their own region, in the name of development.

Notes

1. Various terms are used for this attempt, including "appropriate tourism," "responsible tourism," "small-scale tourism," "green tourism," and "gentle tourism" (Ishimori 1990: 77).
2. According to a 1994 report, attempts were being made to preserve Balinese tradition (*Bali aga*) dating from before the arrival of Hinduism, and Tenganan and Trunyan were being added to the list of tourist villages (Universitas Gadjah Mada 1994).
3. As mentioned in note 2 of chapter 5, Balinese villages are of two types: administrative villages, which are part of the government's administrative system, and customary villages based on traditional custom. Penglipuran is an administrative village belonging to the Kubu division of Bangli district, Bangli regency, but it also forms a single independent customary village, and the customary headman is called the *kelian adat*. The village is described by Kagami and myself in a co-authored article (Yamashita and Kagami 1995).
4. This pattern of regional development based on the participation of the residents is probably also related to the issue of local autonomy that is being promoted in present-day Indonesia, with the devolution of various functions of central government to the regions.

Part III

Beyond Bali

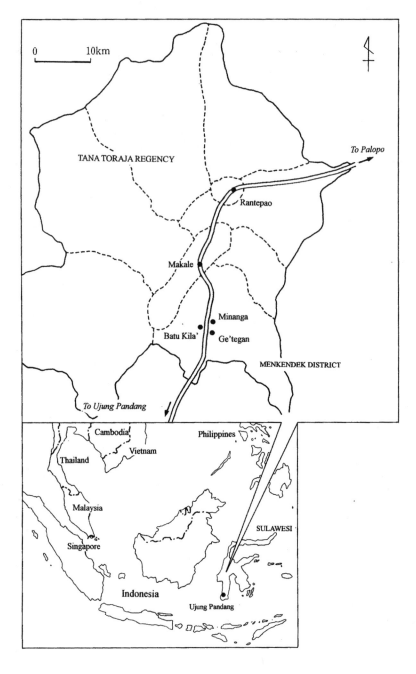

Map 9.1. Tana Toraja.

112

Chapter 9

Manipulating Ethnic Tradition: Tourism

Among the Toraja of Indonesia

In the next three chapters I move away from Bali, and explore the theme of tourism and the production of culture in three different places. The first is the case of the Toraja who live in the mountainous areas of Sulawesi in Indonesia. I analyze the nature of contemporary Toraja ethnic "tradition" using a series of events that took place at a funeral in 1992. At the same time, I also want to look at the ways in which traditional culture is manipulated within the context of the growth of tourism.[1]

1. Tana Toraja

Tana Toraja, or Torajaland, is located about 300 kilometers to the north of Ujung Pandang, also known as Makassar,[2] the capital of South Sulawesi province, in highlands 800 to 1,600 meters in altitude. This is the home of the Toraja people, and the population of the regency is about 340,000. The main occupation is rice cultivation on hillside terraces. There is little industry in the regency apart from a coffee plantation opened in 1977 as a joint venture between Indonesia and Japan. Many people – including many of the youth – therefore migrate in search of work to Ujung Pandang, Jakarta, and the other cities of Indonesia.

The funeral ritual described here was that of Puang Mengkendek, which took place in October and November of 1992. When I carried out my initial fieldwork, from 1976–78, he was the regent. I stayed at his mother's house located at Minanga, a village in the southern district of Mengkendek. This meant that I saw the funeral not so much as something to be observed, but as something in which I was deeply involved. In the following I present a description of the funeral of Puang Mengkendek, followed by an analysis. The focus goes beyond ethnic cultural tradition as something which simply continues, to that which is manipulated and staged, especially in the context of development in contemporary Toraja.

2. The funeral of Puang Mengkendek

Puang Mengkendek, also known as J.K. Andilolo', died of a heart attack in a hospital in Ujung Pandang in December, 1991, at the age of 62. He was from an aristocratic Toraja family: his father, Puang Mengkendek Senior, was Puang or "Lord" of the former Mengkendek kingdom in the southern part of the regency, while his mother, Puang Minanga, was the daughter of Puang Andilolo' of the former Makale kingdom. Thus the title "Puang Mengkendek" was inherited from his father.[3] In 1906 the Dutch colonial government seized control of this region. There were formerly three small kingdoms in the southern part of what is now Tana Toraja, and Mengkendek was one of them, along with Makale and Sangalla'.

Puang Menkengdek had a military career, by the end of which he had risen to the rank of colonel. In 1974 he was appointed as regent of Tana Toraja, in which position he served two terms until 1984. After his retirement he went to live in Ujung Pandang. He served as advisor to the regency from 1984–85, and in 1987 he was elected as a member of the South Sulawesi provincial assembly, in which he remained until his death. After his death, it was decided in a family meeting that the funeral would be held in September, 1992, in his home district of Mengkendek in Tana Toraja. Even though he had been a Protestant, it would be carried out according to Toraja traditional custom. This decision was not unusual: Toraja Christians today take the position that they follow Christianity in their beliefs, but as Toraja they make use of traditional custom.

According to Toraja traditional custom, the way a funeral is carried out is determined by the social status of the deceased and the economic resources available to the family. For this reason, funerals are a way of demonstrating social status, rather than being simply rituals to bury the dead. Generally, it is possible to gain social prestige and reputation through the performance of a lavish ritual; and particularly when rich aristocrats put on magnificent funerals for the sake of prestige and to maintain their social status. The scale of the ritual is measured in terms of the number of water buffalo sacrificed. Among the Toraja, the water buffalo is still the basic measure of wealth, and so sacrifice is a form of conspicuous consumption. At the funeral of a person of high status, there is a huge celebration involving the whole of village society, together with various offerings of buffalo and pigs. In the case of Puang Mengkendek, it was decided to hold the highest rank of funeral celebration known as *diapa'i* as a mark of his aristocratic status and family wealth.

In February 1992, I received an initial letter from Sampe (a pseudonym), Puang Mengkendek's oldest son. In this letter informed me of his father's death, and to say that he wanted me to take part in the funeral ritual "as a member of the family." He also asked me, if possible, to make contact with a Japanese television company: Puang Mengkendek's funeral would be of a magnificence previously unknown in Toraja funerals, marked by the sacrifice of hundreds of buffalo and countless pigs. It would be an enormous spectacle. I did know a television company which was interested in filming a Toraja funeral, and I promptly introduced it to Sampe. Soon a letter arrived from Sampe asking the television company for U.S.$125,000 for the film rights. In fact, this was no more than a first bargaining proposal, and the bargaining over the film rights continued until just before the television company staff arrived in Toraja. Up to then foreign television companies had filmed Toraja funerals as documentaries, but to my knowledge, this was the first occasion on which a payment for the film rights had been requested. Eventually the television company paid Sampe a much smaller honorarium.

It is true that mounting a lavish Toraja funeral involves great expense. The total cost of an earlier large funeral ritual, in 1978, was estimated at around 90 million rupiah, 37,500,000 yen or U.S.$120,000 at the exchange rate at that time. This is the cost if everything is calculated in money terms, but in fact Puang Mengkendek's funeral did not only involve the use of cash. What was actually consumed was rice, buffalo, pigs, and bamboo. Moreover, all the relatives of the bereaved helped share the burden. Thus the Toraja funeral is still basically a social affair, but in recent years cash has become more necessary as a result of the spread of the market economy in Indonesia. The fact that Sampe had looked for contacts with a Japanese television company in order to "sell" his father's funeral was a result of this process.

Most Toraja are peasants, but Sampe is an entrepreneur. He owns a chopstick factory and a food processing plant in Ujung Pandang, and is also involved in the management of a retail trading company. In addition, he was involved in the management of a new hotel which had just opened in Toraja. Moving into business is one way in which the former Toraja aristocracy is attempting to adapt to contemporary Indonesian society. Sampe's hotel is one of a number run by a powerful Jakarta-based hotel group, and he inherited his managerial interest from his late father.[4] When I visited Toraja in October, 1992, the bulk of the hotel was still under construction, but part of it had been completed and had begun to function. In Sampe's mind, the performance of his father's funeral may have been connected to the promotion of his new hotel.

Puang Mengkendek died in Ujung Pandang, and a simple temporary burial was carried out there. Later the remains were taken to Toraja, and laid to rest in his house at Batu Kila' in Mengkendek district. In the case of a large Toraja funeral that requires preparation, a long period – several years in some instances – may elapse before the start of the ritual, and the corpse is normally kept at the family house. In addition, Puang Mengkendek's wife had died in Ujung Pandang in March, 1990. As her funeral had not yet been performed in her homeland, she was buried in a Christian graveyard in Ujung Pandang. Thus Puang Mengkendek's funeral was to be performed as a double funeral for both husband and wife. Coincidentally, during the preparations for the funeral in June, 1992, Puang Mengkendek's second son also died after a sudden illness, so the funeral was now to be performed for all three members of the Andilolo' family.

3. The performance of the funeral

Puang Mengkendek's funeral, which had been scheduled for September, 1992, actually started at the end of October. According to Sampe, the postponement was for the convenience of government officials from Jakarta who were due to attend. I arrived at Ujung Pandang on 25 October, together with the television team. The following day, 26 October, the bodies of Puang Mengkendek's wife and second son were exhumed, and in the evening the coffins were transported to Torajaland, accompanied by a cortege of vehicles containing family members. The next morning we left for Torajaland with the remaining family members. In Torajaland, Puang Mengkendek's body had already been moved from the house at Batu Kila' to the *tongkonan* or "ancestral house," a traditional building with a roof shaped like a boat, two kilometers away at Minanga. When we arrived at Minanga on 27 October, the coffin, which was laid out in the *tongkonan* and wrapped in a red cloth, was being decorated by the goldsmiths with various motifs in gold leaf. The same thing was being done to the coffins of his wife and second son in the house at Batu Kila'.

The funeral began on 30 October. Puang Mengkendek's decorated coffin left the *tongkonan*, and was moved to a space in one of the rice barns built

Figure 9.1. Toraja funerals. Carrying the *sarigan*,
shaped like a traditional roof.

opposite (there were four of these in all). At the same time, the coffins of his
wife and son were brought from Batu Kila', and laid in a space in the barn.
Four buffalo were sacrificed, and their meat distributed. The coffins remained
there for three nights, while the family of the deceased watched over them,
bewailing the separation. In addition to bamboo flute (*suling*) music, a la-
ment called the *marakka'* was sung, and villagers performed a dirge called
the *ma'badong*. In this they sing about the life of the deceased, and send off
his spirit to the other world, but it is also for the enjoyment of the villagers.

Three days later, on 2 November, the coffins of Puang Mengkendek, his
wife and his son, were taken from Minanga to the ceremonial field, which
had been prepared at Ge'tegan four kilometers away, accompanied by a festive funeral procession. The procession consisted of dancing warriors called
to maranding who acted as guides; several dozen water buffalo; the coffins,
carried by a large number of men on frames called *sarigan*, made in the
shape of traditional roofs (rather like Japanese *mikoshi* or portable shrines);
effigies of the deceased called *tau-tau*; water buffalo with decorated horns;
the men and women of the family; and the villagers. In addition to the im-
pressive procession, the atmosphere was festive. When the bodies arrived at
the ceremonial ground they were placed in the *lakkean*, a small hut in the
center. The focus of the ritual had now moved to the ceremonial ground,

where a large number of people gathered. A bullfight called *tedong silaga* took place between water buffalo. When night fell, the mourners made offerings of pigs, prepared a kind of food called *pa'piong* in bamboo tubes (the traditional Toraja food on ritual occasions). They consumed quantities of meat, drank palm wine, and enjoyed the music of the *ma'badong*.

The three days from 3 to 5 November were devoted to the reception of people who came to pay their respects. These included distinguished visitors from Jakarta and Ujung Pandang; the aristocrats from the former Buginese kingdom of Bone; officials and the women's association of Tana Toraja; relatives living both in and outside the area; and ordinary villagers. They were divided into groups of 20 to 100 people, and they moved in procession across the ceremonial ground. The visitors brought with them water buffalo, pigs, palm wine, and, in some cases, cash. Their condolence gifts were carefully recorded, as they were a debt that would have to be repaid later. A reception hut was prepared for these visitors in the center of the ceremonial ground, and they were entertained there with coffee, cigarettes and cakes. This was repeated over and over again. During this period, 334 groups of visitors paid their respects, bringing 48 buffalo and 254 pigs.

On 6 November, the "day of sacrifice," many buffalo were slaughtered, and their meat was distributed to the villages concerned. In part this ritual was a thank offering to the villages that had helped with the funeral arrangements, in return for their cooperation, but the large-scale sacrifice of buffalo is also a form of conspicuous consumption. However, not all the buffalo were killed, and some were presented live. Taking meat to distant villages was difficult given that it would rot over time. The live buffalo could be sold for cash in the village, and so could contribute to village development. Offerings of a total of 60 buffalo were made during the funeral, including the live ones that were given away.

On 7 November, the bodies were buried. Traditionally among the Toraja bodies were buried in *liang*, stone graves made in limestone cliffs. However, today, Christians are usually buried in the ground, and Puang Mengkendek's body was buried in a family graveyard on the hill behind the house at Batu Kila'. The burial ritual honored him as an army colonel, and was carried out in military style, with the local army division participating.

4. Analysis

Here I consider four major points: (a) labor migration and religion; (b) changes in Toraja traditional religion; (c) tourism and the transition from ritual to festivals; and (d) the manipulation and presentation of tradition.

(a) Labor migration and religion

In Tana Toraja there are no industries to absorb the local population increase, no areas suitable for the development of new farmland, and no universities for further education. As a result, many people today are leaving the home-land mountain villages and heading for the cities such as Ujung Pandang and Jakarta as labor migrants. According to some estimates, the number of Toraja who have moved out is around 230,000 (Volkman 1990: 93). This practice of migration is called *merantau* in Indonesian. Of Puang Mengkendek's ten children, only two remain in Tana Toraja regency: most of them live in Ujung Pandang or Jakarta. According to the condolence list from his funeral, about 20 percent of the visitors came from the various cities to which they had migrated. I have described elsewhere, based on my previous research in Ujung Pandang, the mutual interdependence of homeland village society and the urban society to which people have moved (Yamashita 1986). In the perfor-mance of ritual as well, present-day Toraja village society can only be under-stood by taking migrant urban society into account.

It is important to consider the religious problems that are caused as people leave their home villages to find work in distant urban areas. Living in cities with people around who are very different socially and culturally, Toraja migrants are unable practice their traditional religion in the same way as before. In the case of the Toraja in Ujung Pandang, they maintain their ethnic identity in the form of belief in Christianity. Many of the Toraja choose Chris-tianity in opposition to the "sea of Islam" consisting of the Bugis and Makassar majority in the city. In Sumatra, Borneo and the Malay peninsula there has been a pattern in which people who convert to Islam become "Malay" (Obayashi 1984: 14; Kipp and Rodgers 1987: 4), but the Toraja reinforce their own ethnic identity by choosing Christianity instead.[5]

Historically, the Toraja encounter with Christianity can be traced back to 1913 when a Dutch Reform Church minister arrived there. Up to the 1950s, however, only about 10 percent of the local people had converted. Until this time converts were generally younger members of the ruling class who were educated at mission schools. The reason why a larger number of people con-verted was the development of a fundamentalist Islamic movement in South Sulawesi in the 1950s, during which the Toraja turned to Christianity be-cause it was a religion opposed to Islam. By the time of my first fieldwork, in 1976–78, about 60 percent of the local people had become Christians, and today this has risen to around 80 percent.[6]

(b) Changes in traditional religion

Labor migration and conversion to Christianity do not necessarily mean that the Toraja have abandoned their traditions. For instance, people go home for the sake of a lavish funeral, as in the case of Puang Mengkendek, and in their homeland they stress Toraja custom rather than Christian beliefs. Indeed, conversion to Christianity did not mean casting off Toraja customs, in particular, the offerings of pigs and buffalo at funerals. Offerings are not only linked to religious ideas of sending the soul of the dead to the other world, but are also inseparable from the social element of prestige, and the economic element of the division of the inheritance, and so cannot be abandoned. The Christianization of the Toraja also means the Torajanization of Christianity.

In addition, since the end of the 1970s, as I describe below, traditional culture has been reconsidered against the background of the development of tourism. Christianity has also made creative use of the staging of traditional ritual as Toraja custom in the performance of lavish Christian-style "traditional" funerals with the money earned from working in the city. Here, the enlargement of Toraja society, which has occurred along with labor migration to urban areas, is actually linked to the preservation and reinforcement of "traditional" culture.

Toraja traditional religion is called Aluk To Dolo', the "way of the ancestors." By nature it is a practical religion in contrast to the scriptural religions, and a communal religion in contrast to the religions of salvation. As I have discussed previously, Aluk To Dolo' originated in rituals of birth and death (Yamashita 1988: 131-153), but – according to the Toraja – rather than being a narrow religion in this sense, it is conceived of as similar to Pierre Bourdieu's concept of *habitus*: customary behavior, which has been structured as part of the unconscious (Bourdieu 1977: 72). Incidentally, Toraja Aluk To Dolo' was recognized in 1969 by the Indonesian government as a sect of "Hinduism." As I noted in chapter 5, religion (*agama*) in Indonesia is officially regulated, and the *panca sila* (the five principles of nation-building) explain the minimal definition as "belief in one God." Islam, Christianity, Hinduism, Confucianism and Buddhism are therefore recognized as *agama* by the government, but others are not. Aluk To Dolo' was previously treated as "animism," which the Indonesian Ministry of Religion does not recognize, but now it is seen as a Hindu sect.[7] This decision was connected in complicated ways with the regional development of tourism which focused on the Toraja religious tradition (Yamashita 1988: 12-14).

However, most of the believers in Aluk To Dolo' are old, and their number is getting smaller every year with the passing of the generations. At the time of my 1976–78 research, they formed about 30 percent of the local population, but now they form only 10 percent and are still decreasing. As I mentioned before, the Christians form a majority in the regency, with 80 percent of the population. Muslims form a minority in Toraja, with about 10 percent. Against the background of these changes in the structure of religion in local society, Aluk To Dolo' as a communal religion is in danger of falling apart. First, the reciprocal social and economic relationships that supported Aluk To Dolo' still exist, but no longer constitute a community based on shared beliefs. In Toraja today, many people are believers in Christianity. Secondly, people are becoming alienated from Aluk To Dolo' as a form of *habitus*, which is internalized in the unconscious. For instance, among the families who have migrated to the city and who came back for Puang Mengkendek's funeral, there are many who think of the "Toraja way" as boring, meaningless, and sometimes painful. The food made in bamboo tubes known as *pa'piong* is the normal food for ritual occasions, but it no longer suits the tastes of a proportion of urban migrants; so that in the cooking huts, people were also cooking things like stir-fried vegetables and deep-fried fish, which are not traditional Toraja cuisine. Even Sampe, the chief mourner, did not stay at the funeral place, but returned to his own hotel by car, and instead of joining in with the *ma'badong*, he entertained himself with *karaoke* in the hotel lobby. The religious tradition of the Toraja who undertake rituals is undergoing a great change from within.

(c) Tourism and the transition from ritual to festivals

As a communal religion, Toraja religion is breaking down, but the religious tradition today is also being reborn under new conditions, that is to say, within the context of tourism. Here, what was once religious ritual is becoming a spectacle to be viewed by tourists (cf. Acciaioli 1985). In Toraja a tourism development policy was introduced by the government in the 1970s, and as a result the number of foreign tourists rose from only 58 in 1971 to nearly 25,000 in 1977, increasing to around 40,000 in 1990.[8]

Tourism in Toraja is a type of "ethnic tourism." It focuses on exotic customs, and includes visits to the houses and villages of the local people, watching dances and rituals, and the purchase of unusual "primitive" souvenirs (Smith 1977: 2). In the case of the Toraja, the focus is their unique ethnic culture, and especially the funerals with their large-scale sacrifice of water buffalo.

Figure 9.2. Toraja hotel, built in traditional *tongkonan* style.

Puang Mengkendek's funeral was a Christian version of the highest rank of funeral ritual known as *diapa'i*. Today, the number of adherents of Aluk To Dolo' is decreasing, and many of the "traditional" rituals that the tourists see are the Christian versions. Therefore, in what is now rather a general phenomenon, the rituals the tourists photograph as "traditional" and "authentic" are actually performed by Christians, and are made possible by the money earned through migrant labor. The Christian funeral is an abridged and simplified version of a number of elements drawn from the complex procedure of the authentic traditional ritual, which make sense according to Christian beliefs. In this version, the spectacle has been emphasized in addition to the social aspects. For instance, the sacrifices are not a religious act from the Christian point of view, but are socially significant. In other words, Christianity does not recognize the belief that the animals are sacrificed to conduct the soul of the deceased to the other world: according to the Christians, the meat from the offerings is shared by the local society. The sacrifices are therefore reduced to a sociological phenomenon that contributes to social solidarity. In addition, the sacrifices, and especially those of the buffalo, are a dramatic spectacle that may also be seen as a reflection of strange, shocking, "primitive" customs, especially by the tourists. The Toraja *habitus* is transformed under the tourist gaze into an object of curiosity.

Plate 9.3. Souvenirs in the style of funeral effigies (*tau tau*).

As Katherine Adams has analyzed, the tourist industry is a broker for ethnicity, creating ethnic stereotypes by selecting ethnic markers, simplifying them, exaggerating them, and circulating them as commodities (Adams 1984). One prominent ethnic marker among the Toraja is the *tongkonan*, the ancestral house with its boat-shaped roof, and this is greatly emphasized in relation to tourism. The local government promotes and subsidizes the construction of *tongkonan* by the local residents for the benefit of the tourists who come to see these unique roofs. They have also been built for the use of tourists, and many of the Toraja hotels make use of as pastiche of *tongkonan* construction motifs. *Tongkonan* models are sold as souvenirs, and T-shirts and carvings have *tongkonan* designs. "Pastiche" is a key concept in postmodernism, according to Frederik Jameson (1983), but here the copy has taken on more life than the real thing, and the real thing has lost its meaning.

Actually a *tongkonan* is not necessarily a comfortable place to live for Toraja today. The windows are too small and let in insufficient light. The structures are too narrow and inconvenient for contemporary lifestyles. For this reason, as a compromise, some *tongkonan* houses are being converted with the addition of a Buginese-style extension, while others are abandoned or are only built for the tourists. Puang Mengkendek's *tongkonan* at Minanga was built in 1968, but his mother lived in a brick house built next to it. In

Figure 9.4. Tourists watching funeral ritual.

fact, apart from myself and my wife, who lived there during our fieldwork, nobody ever lived in this "ancestral house."

The funeral of Puang Mengkendek provided the tourists with a number of spectacles. They obtained photographs and videos of the water buffalo being sacrificed, the people with their traditional costumes, and the circular funeral dance. In this way, culture is cut off from society in the context of tourism, and it becomes an object for aesthetic appreciation or consumption. Nelson Graburn has discussed the affinity of the tourist and the artistic gaze (Graburn 1989: 24). Under this type of gaze, the *tongkonan* becomes an example of artistic architecture rather than the seat of the ancestors, and the funeral becomes an aesthetic object to be photographed.[9]

(d) The manipulation and staging of tradition

Puang Mengkendek's eldest son, Sampe, who played the role of the chief mourner, was not a Christian, but rather a Muslim, because he had married a Muslim woman from Northern Sulawesi. The funeral for the Christian Puang Mengkendek was carried out by his Muslim son using traditional Toraja custom – an interesting combination however you look at it. To Sampe, the fact that his religion was different from that of his father lost its significance in the face of Toraja custom. However, the custom here has ceased to be unconscious *habitus* and is understood as consciously constructed tradition. Tradition in this context is not custom embedded in Toraja society, but is something removed from its social matrix that becomes the object of manipulation in the context of reawakened consciousness. In manipulating and staging tradition, Sampe also saw things as an outsider even though he was Toraja. Through the experience of migration, the Toraja cannot avoid seeing things in more complex ways. With the development of tourism taking place, the tourist gaze must have an influence on the way in which the Toraja see their own culture.

Toraja tourism focuses particularly on funerals, and so Sampe saw his father's funeral as a perfect opportunity to promote both Toraja tourism and his new hotel. For this reason he invited officials from Jakarta, including a minister, and the president of the hotel group to which Sampe's hotel belonged. The minister did not come, but the president did; he was led to a specially prepared VIP seat, and was treated as the most important of those paying their respects. As a businessman, Sampe made the most of this opportunity, and the fact that he presented Toraja culture to important guests from the Indonesian center was extremely important. (Recently, the scale of Toraja funerals has been assessed not so much in terms of the numbers of buffalo sacrificed, but rather in terms of the number of ministers attending from Jakarta.)

At Puang Mengkendek's funeral there was also the Japanese television company that came to film it. For Sampe, television meant the promotion of Toraja tourism, and especially the hotel as one of his enterprises, in addition to being a record of the ritual carried out in honor of his father. On the other hand, to the television company the Toraja funeral was a custom that would arouse the curiosity of the viewers in the "primitive." The company's prospectus for the program about the funeral depicted it as a drama of human life and death, a "ritual overflowing with the blood of animal sacrifice," and suggested that Japanese who seldom come into direct contact with death would find it shocking. On location, one of the granddaughters of the deceased who had been brought up in the city of Ujung Pandang returned home for the funeral. The television director considered a story line, which depicted the traditional Toraja funeral seen through the eyes of the granddaughter, comparing it with life in the city. However, the girl who was to be the heroine (Sampe's eldest daughter) did not behave as the television director had anticipated. Having been brought up in the city, and with a mother who was not Toraja, she seemed alienated from the rituals, and did not want to take part in the "primitive" Toraja funeral scenes.

Eventually, the program was edited in a style which presented the Toraja funeral material systematically from start to finish. The newspaper blurb on the day of the broadcast introduced it under the title of "Toraja! Festival of death, the people who live to die," with a succession of phrases such as "Indonesia's biggest funeral of the century lasting nine days," "A ritual with 50,000 guests and the sacrifice of 500 buffalo and pigs," and "Pork cooked in bamboo tubes."[10] A buffalo herdsman was selected for the leading part in this "drama of life and death." The focus of the drama was a sentimental story about the buffalo boy, and his sadness when his buffalo was chosen for sacrifice. This sentimentalism was the result of the film being edited with the Japanese audience in mind, and it had nothing to do with the viewpoint of the Toraja.

At any rate, like tourism, television today is a powerful medium for presenting images of ethnic culture. In this case, the presentation of the image was repeatedly underpinned by an ideology of the "pristine" original culture which present-day society has lost. In order to create this image, television even makes things up. However, the point is that this is not only the ideology of a television company. Like Sampe in Puang Mengkendek's funeral, the Toraja can also make use of television. This means that today, there are two ways of manipulating and staging ethnic culture: for the Toraja, and for the media.

5. Tourism and cultural differentiation

The force of globalization and the disappearance of boundaries are being felt even in Toraja, despite its relatively marginal position within Indonesia. In this context, in order to understand Puang Mengkendek's funeral, which I have discussed in this chapter, we need a framework that goes beyond Toraja, to include the viewpoints of the Indonesian nation, foreign tourists, and even foreign television and other media. In this context, traditional Toraja religion, which was once embedded in society, is decomposed into its elements, such as beliefs, customs, and arts. Today these various elements are reset in a delicate balance, and are being re-created or reconstructed. This is not a process of religious secularization accompanying modernization, or the rationalization of religion. Instead it shows the way in which cultural tradition can exist within the context of tourism.

Notes

1. An earlier version of this paper was published in English as Yamashita (1994c).
2. In 1999 the name of the city of Ujung Pandang was changed to Makassar, which was actually the old name of the city before 1971. In this book, I continue to use the name Ujung Pandang, which was current at the time of research.
3. According to a booklet on Puang Andilolo', he succeeded to this title in 1947 (Andilolo' 1992: 2). However, I never heard of him using this title during his lifetime.
4. This was a typical case of a situation common under the Suharto regime, that of a politician and his family members also being involved in business – Suharto's own family being the most prominent example.
5. For an example of Christianity being chosen in opposition to the religion of the people of the plains, or as an ethnic identity marker among the Aka in the mountain areas of Myanmar and Thailand, see the account by Kammerer (1990). The recent Aka acceptance of Christianity appears to be a way of marking the boundary with the Buddhist majority in the plains who also, to some extent, retain Aka ethnic identity (1990: 277). This account has many similarities with the Toraja in relation to traditional religion and ethnic identity, and the pattern of conversion to Christianity.
6. The majority of Toraja Christians are Protestants, belonging to the Toraja Church, which is a branch of the Dutch Reform Church, but there are also Catholics and followers of the newer Protestant denominations, such as the Pentacostalists and Seventh Day Adventists.
7. On the issues of *agama* (religion) that are peculiar to Indonesia, see Fukushima (1991). In relation to Bali, see chapter 4 above.
8. In 1990, a report to the Toraja regional assembly on the master plan for the development of Toraja tourism predicted 360,000 tourists a year by 2010, and proposed the development of the facilities required for a real international tourist destination, and the construction of the infrastructure to receive them.
9. It should probably be added that today it is not only the tourists, but also the Toraja, who photograph and video their own funerals.
10. *Asahi Shimbun*, January 25, 1992.

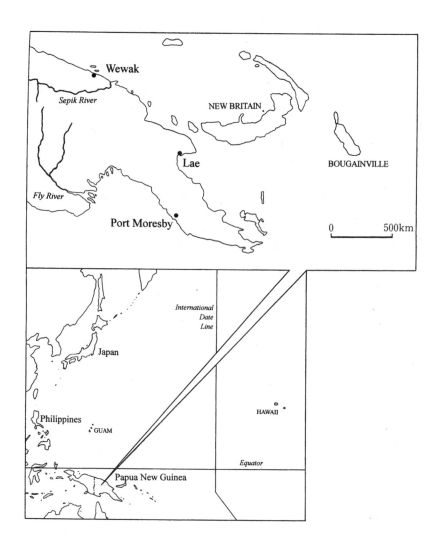

Map 10.1 Papua New Guinea: Sepik River Region

Chapter 10

The *"Cannibal Tours"* Adventure:

Sepik River Tourism in Papua New Guinea

"Cannibal Tours" is a film made by the Australian film maker, Dennis O'Rourke. It deals with tourism in the Sepik River region of Papua New Guinea – where cannibalism is said to have happened in the past – and provides some very interesting insights into "ethnic tourism."[1] In this chapter, through a discussion of the film, I investigate the problems that this kind of tourism entails.

1. *"Cannibal Tours"*

First I want to review briefly the points made in the film.[2] Thirty thousand tourists a year visit Papua New Guinea. This film features Western tourists (Germans, Americans and Italians) on a luxury cruise ship, the *Melanesian Explorer*, complete with air conditioning and catering, chatting as they sail up the Sepik River – "Eggs have cholesterol. But no calories"; "The crocodiles are sunning themselves in the jungle." The background music consists of Mozart, elegantly played. The tourists visit the villages along the river, and visit *haus tambaran* or spirit-houses, a focal point of Sepik tourism. However, in this village, as an old man explains,

> All of the sacred objects, the Germans took them, the English and Australians took them – everything. There is nothing left here. The missionaries destroyed all the most powerful symbols kept in the spirit-house, the ancient things which we would hide here. The missionaries threw them out, saying, "It's the Devil! Get rid of it!"

Today the spirit-houses are built for the tourists to photograph, paying about U.S.$2 per camera.

Another focus is carving, the best-known craft in the area. The tourists haggle over the carvings that the village people lay out. These bargaining negotiations make the local people annoyed. In the words of a village elder,

> What I ask for my carvings is what I should be paid. People should pay me the money that I ask. I don't agree with "second price" and "third price." I want them to pay me without any fuss my own small amount of money. But they ask for "second price" and "third price." It's wrong, because when I go to those big shops in the town, I can't buy things for "second price" or "third price." I must pay the first price.

And in the words of a woman trader, directing her resentment at the tourists,

> We hurry down here with things for the tourists but the tourists only look, they don't buy. These tourists come, but they don't really help us. How is it that the tourists have money, but not us? We have nothing. See my children who must go to school? What happens when I can't sell these things?

On the other hand, the tourists say that bargaining is expected and they enjoy the negotiations. But one of the tourists also commented on the relationship between tourism and art as follows:

> Well, one of my primary interests in life is primitive art. . . [There were] many [television] programs devoted to the art of this area, and I said to myself, I won't rest short of going to New Guinea myself. And actually I have fortunately found what I was looking for in terms of their art – [but] I for one feel that it is too bad if they then deviate from it and work for tourism as such.

The tourists take a great number of photographs and videos, posing with the local people, for which they certainly pay their models. Taking photographs is one of the most important themes of the film, and it persistently highlights scenes of tourists taking photographs. The local people know well that the tourists pay to take photos, while they take the money.

In relation to historical relations with Europeans, a Sepik village elder gives the following account: "We were not born – it was our parents who

Figure 10.1. Tourists with painted faces. (From *"Cannibal Tours,"* 1987, photograph by Dennis O'Rourke.)

saw the first Europeans. Everyone was afraid; they said, 'Our dead ancestors have returned. The spirits of our dead have come back!' So now when we see tourists, we say about them: 'The dead have returned!'"[3] About conflict, he says, "I'll tell you about how we would fight. We would cut off heads, remove the skin, and then eat. The Germans came but white men were no different. We fought them too. We killed one of them. They killed many of us and burnt our houses." About the tourists, he says,

> All that we know is that [the tourists] are from another country. We sit here confused, while they take pictures of everything. They do give us a little money if they go inside the spirit house. We don't understand why these foreigners take photographs. . . Before we didn't have money. Then we gained independence – now we have a little money. And we only get money by selling our carvings. If they don't buy our carvings we have no money. And the money we get for our carvings – it doesn't last.

He then smiles and adds, "If they paid me more, I could go on that ship with the tourists!"

Towards the end of the film there is a scene in which the tourists enjoy painting themselves with body paint like the Papuans, playing at going "primitive" themselves.[4]

2. Power relations in tourism

First of all, the film shows that this sort of tourism is based on unequal power relations, within which the tourists are "civilized" people who come from the "wealthy North," and their hosts – the "primitive" people of the "poor South," i.e. Papua New Guinean "relics from the stone age" – are burdened with them. The opposition between the "civilized" and the "primitive" reappears in relation to tourism, colored by the North-South problem. This situation is shown clearly in the words of the angry local woman selling souvenirs:

> You white people! You have all the money! We village people have no money. You've got money, not us "backward" people! That's why I complain. I'm talking about these things here [pointing to the handicrafts which include ironically Melanesian shell money] and tourists ignore them. They don't buy from us, and it's a problem!

An interesting conversation takes place near the opening of the film between a German being guided round a former cannibal location and his guide: "Where have they killed people? Here? Let's go and see. Right there? People got killed here? Now I need a photograph. The two of us at this stone – for the memory. It would be nice." But what on earth is he going to remember, and why is he taking the photograph? What the photograph symbolizes here is a kind of "primitivism" analogous to "Orientalism" in the West from which the tourists come, that is to say the way in Westerners perceive or construct "the Orient." The construction of "primitives" by the "civilized" through the viewfinders of their cameras was already happening in the nineteenth century, as Sontag says:

> After the opening of the West in 1869 by the completion of the transcontinental railroad came the colonization through photography. The case of the American Indians is the most brutal. Discreet, serious amateurs like Vroman had been operating since the end of the Civil War. They were the vanguard of an army of tourists who arrived by the end of the century, eager for a good shot of Indian life. The tourists invaded the Indians' privacy, photographing holy objects and the sacred dances and places, if

necessary paying the Indians to pose and getting them to revise their ceremonies to provide more photogenic material. (Sontag 1979: 64-65)

Today, when anthropologists debate the question of the "primitive" and whether it is a fiction created by the modern West, the tourists continue to recreate "primitives" in the viewfinders of their cameras. As O'Rourke who made the film says,

> In *"Cannibal Tours"* there are two journeys. The first is what the film depicts, that of rich tourists on a luxury cruise up the mysterious Sepik River, and enjoying the packaged "heart of darkness" of the New Guinea jungle. The other is what might be called a metaphysical journey (in fact this is the text of the film), which attempts to reveal the place of the "other" in the human imagination. (MacCannell 1992: 25)

However, as the film shows, the primitive does not exist. What exists are people who were formerly "primitive," or people playing the role of "primitives." In playing a role within the power relations in the world today, there is a problem of stereotyped representation. The process by which the "normal life" of the Sepik people becomes the "cannibal tours" of the tourists arises from this. Today's tourism cannot avoid these political problems of representation. Tourism therefore has often been seen as a new form of colonialism. Nevertheless, why do the Sepik people allow tourism? The villagers in the film say that it is because of money. Of course the tourists encounter people of a different cultural background under peaceful conditions, and this is one form of interaction with them. As tourism today is a type of commodity, interaction with tourists remains basically an economic transaction. Tourists are buying something out of the ordinary and consuming it, and the host people are selling it.[5]

3. Photographs and souvenirs as copies of the tourist experience

In the film, tourists are portrayed as taking large numbers of photographs and buying souvenirs. I have touched on one aspect of this above, but another aspect is that taking photographs is how the tourists authenticate their own experiences. Probably many of the tourists could not imagine going on a trip without a camera. As Sontag says, "It seems positively unnatural to travel for pleasure without taking a camera along. Photographs will offer indisputable evidence that the trip was made, that the program was carried out, that fun was had" (Sontag 1979: 9). However, tourists often set up their cameras before they actually look at anything, and after they have pressed the shutter they do not look at anything else. This means that the experience of travel is something that takes place later, when the pictures are developed. To quote Sontag again, "A way of certifying experience, taking photographs is also a way of refusing it – by limiting experience to a search for the photogenic, by converting experience into an image, a souvenir." (Sontag 1979: ibid.). Like souvenirs, photographs are a means of giving the illusion that you are experiencing something.

Tourists read the guidebooks before setting out on a trip, they go to the places written up in them, and they take the same kind of photographs of places mentioned in the guidebook. Boorstin's concept of the pseudo-event is also applicable here (Boorstin 1963). As the Sepik elder describes: "With regard to the way we live, I think the tourists read about us in books, and come. Do we still live like our forefathers? Are we civilized or not? They come to find out."

To the tourists, souvenirs are things by which to remember the trip, and they resemble photographs in that they are copies of the trip. Souvenirs, whether they are Sepik carvings or Indonesian batik cloth, are the medium by which the ethnicity of the local cultural group is expressed. Sepik carvings were originally ritual objects, but they are endowed with authenticity by being collected by explorers and valued as "primitive art." As discussed in chapter 3 this is the transformation in value that results from what Clifford calls the "modern art-culture system" (Clifford 1988: 222-26). In the case of the Sepik carvings, "as the ancient art, original to the area, based on aboriginal beliefs, they are valuable both ethnologically and artistically."[6] So they are made and sold as souvenirs, and the tourists buy them in that form as the essence of Sepik ethnicity.

As the souvenirs are bought by the tourists, they transcend ethnic boundaries. Paula Ben-Amos has compared souvenirs with pidgin languages, which are used in trade between peoples who speak different languages because of the necessity of mutual understanding. Both souvenirs and pidgin languages are often used as a means of communication to allow trade between peoples of different cultures, and this involves processes of simplification, standardization, and deviation from tradition (Ben-Amos 1977). Among the characteristics that souvenirs and pidgin languages share, therefore, is this secondary existence.

It is very interesting to consider buying souvenirs as a form of cultural transmission similar to communicating in a pidgin language. Conventional anthropologists have carried out research treating culture as something that functions in societies with definite boundaries. However, in today's "borderless" world, in an age when culture is appreciated beyond social boundaries, it is becoming impossible to treat culture as a bounded system. For instance, staffs made for rituals among the people of the Sepik River are sold as souvenirs, and they decorate the living rooms of German tourists. "Traveling souvenirs" is a useful topic to research in order to observe "traveling culture."

4. Postmodern tourism: the *"Cannibal Tours"* adventure

As already mentioned, this film ends with a scene in which the tourists as a joke, paint themselves with body paint, like the Sepik people. In this scene they are not merely observers, but also participants. If modern tourism is based on the separation between the observers and the observed, in this scene the boundary between the observing guests and the observed hosts wavers and disappears. This vanishing boundary is where the ludic phase of what might be called the postmodern tourism experience is to be found. In *"Cannibal Tours,"* the tourists already know that in New Guinea things like cannibalism no longer exist. To begin with, if cannibalism did exist (and if there were no air-conditioned cruiser) they would probably not go to New Guinea or up the Sepik River. What the tourists really want is to experience going from a safe, "civilized" place to one that is "primitive." What they experience here is not something that is really primitive (insofar as it exists at all), but a reconstructed "primitiveness." As Edward Bruner says, the substance of postmodern tourism is the experience of a copy or simulacrum, and the copy becomes more important than the real thing (Bruner 1989: 438).

Yanagita Kunio, the founder of Japanese folklore studies, once said that he never believed Japanese who see a picture and say that it looks like the real thing, or who see the real thing and say that it looks like a picture (Yanagita 1956: 71). However, it is often the case that a picture (or a photograph, an image, or a copy) may look more real and more beautiful than the real thing. The issue of the representation of the tourist experience is related to this question of the reversal of reality and image. The tourists in *"Cannibal Tours"* thus see a copy of reconstituted primitiveness – or perhaps we should say "hyper-reality," following Jean Baudrillard (1981) – and within this they take photographs, buy souvenirs, and amuse themselves by pretending to be primitive.

The kind of tourists which Maxine Feifer labeled "post-tourists" do not admit that you can experience the real thing. According to them, tourism involves playing a kind of game. Rather than looking for authenticity in the tourist experience, they look for enjoyment in just the opposite. John Urry sees post-tourism as being related to postmodernism in which key concepts are those of simulacrum and hyper-reality (Feifer 1985; Urry 1990: 82-103). If the real thing is compared with a copy, probably the majority of people would say that the real thing is better. However, I think that seeing the copy as second-rate and admiring the original is a modern way of thinking. According to Fredric Jameson (1983), the key concept in the postmodern era is "pastiche." When the adventure in search of the primitive is seen from the point of view of pastiche, *"Cannibal Tours"* is not simply a depiction of Sepik tourism in New Guinea, but also a brilliant representation of one aspect of contemporary postmodern culture.

Notes

1. The film was made by O'Rourke & Associates: Filmmakers, GPO Box 199, Canberra, Australia 2601. For O'Rourke's own commentary on the film, see O'Rourke 1997. For Japanese images of Sepik tourism, see the issue of *Chikyû no arukikata* on Papua New Guinea (Diamondsha 1991, p. 96). In this, under the headline "A Challenging Adventure in the Wilds: the Sepik River Region," the blurb states: "This is a region where you can experience real jungle. A journey in which you visit little villages on the river bank while canoeing down the Sepik River that meanders through the tropical forest. This is what an exploration of the wild is all about."

2. A shortened version of the film was broadcast on NHK television on December 9, 1989, in which the original length was reduced from 77 to 45 minutes, and the description here was originally based on the version as seen in Japan. The quotations here are based on the sound track and English subtitles of the original film, in which most of the spoken dialogue was in German, Italian, and Papua New Guinean languages. Much of this dialogue was left out of the Japanese version.

3. In Papua New Guinea in general, the arrival of the Europeans is said to have been the return of mythical figures or departed ancestors (Schieffelin and Crittenden 1991: 3). This is perhaps related to the myth of the "stranger-king" (Sahlins 1993: chap. 3, Yamashita 1994a.).

4. To reinforce this, the original version of the film ends with a scene in which a woman tourist clambers into a Cessna airplane carrying a bundle of carved phalluses as souvenirs.

5. Deborah Gewertz and Frederick Errington discuss the contradictions in initiation ceremonies becoming the object of tourism among the Chamberi of the Sepik River area of New Guinea, i.e. between the tourists who want to see the undeveloped Chamberi, and the Chamberi who are trying to attract tourists in order to develop (1991: 28). This is the kind of contradiction between economy and culture that *"Cannibal Tours"* also depicts.

6. *Chikyu no arukikata: Papua New Guinea (Guidebook)*, 1991: 96.

Chapter 11

The Home of Folklore: Tourism in Tôno,

Northeastern Japan

Tôno in Iwate Prefecture, Northeastern Japan, is a sparsely populated city of only 30,000 people. However, it has become famous because of the book, *Tôno monogatari* (Tales of Tôno), by Yanagita Kunio, the founding father of Japanese folklore studies. "Folklore tourism" itself has developed on the basis of this book. In this chapter, I discuss tourism in Tôno, and investigate the links between folk culture and tourism in contemporary Japan. I look at how the Tôno tourist industry is attempting to re-appropriate for the local area the folk tales that were previously appropriated – via Yanagita – by metropolitan Japan.

1. Tôno: "the home of folklore"

Tôno was once a post town in the Nambu region of northeastern Japan, which became prosperous through the trade between the inland areas and the coast. However, the city is suffering from depopulation: 80 percent of its area consists of mountain forests, and there is no industry of any importance apart from farming. As in other mountainous areas in the interior of Japan, the younger age groups have declined, and the "graying" of the local population continues. This little city, however, is famous because of the book, *Tôno monogatari* (Tales of Tôno), which consists of folk tales told by Sasaki Kizen, which Yanagita Kunio recorded and published in 1910 (Yanagita 1975). The first edition of the book consisted of only 500 copies, but it later became famous as the work which inspired the birth of Japanese folklore studies.[1] Because of this, scholars concerned with Japanese folklore and ethnology

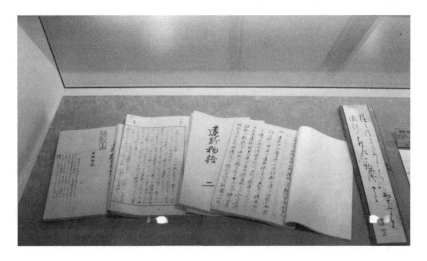

Figure 11.1. Manuscript of Yanagita's *Tôno monogatari* on display in Tôno
City Museum.

began to regard *Tôno monogatari* with almost religious awe. The name of
the town is always associated with the book, and Tôno itself has come to be
regarded as symbolizing Japanese folk culture, along with Yanagita's classic.

While *"Cannibal Tours"* is based on the notion of the exotic as we saw in
the previous chapter, the Tôno tourist industry relies on Japanese nostalgia
for the vanishing world of folklore (Kawamori 1996). Accordingly, Tôno
City presents itself as the "home of folklore." As Ôta Yoshinobu has described, when you get off the train at the JR (Japan Railways) station in
Tôno, on the roundabout straight in front of you is a monument to *Tôno
monogatari*, and an imaginary creature – a *kappa* or water sprite named
Densuke – welcomes you. Tôno thus represents the town described in the
book (Ôta 1993: 392-93). In relation to this fame, however, Ôta cites an
illuminating passage from Iwamoto Yoshiteru's *Mô hitotsu no Tôno
monogatari* (Alternative *Tales of Tôno*), the account given by a taxi driver
(Iwamoto 1983: 14-15). According to the taxi driver, *Tôno monogatari* is
very different from the stories he himself heard from the old people, but if
what he tells the visitors does not correspond to Yanagita's account, the tourists say that his version is no good because of the differences. Now he memo-
rizes the book and bases his account on that.

There is naturally a gap between the image of Tôno in the book and the
reality of the city itself. Asked the reason for visiting the place, one tourist

gave the following answer: "I came after reading Yanagita's *Tôno monogatari*. I thought that the place would be more rural, but when I got to the JR station at Tôno, I was surprised to see a city."[2] Many people who visit the city experience disappointment in the difference between their expectations based on the book – the image of the world of the Japanese mountain villages, with their *kappa* appearing from waterfalls (which Yanagita wrote about "to scare the people who live in the plains")[3] However, Tôno is not a closed mountain village, as was mentioned above, but a post town which developed on the basis of the trade between the inland areas and the coast. As Akasaka Norio says, Tôno is "just an ordinary town." And he continues: "For me, Tôno began when the spell of the place was broken. It has changed just like the other cities and villages in Japan. This means that the only interesting thing about it is the way in which people read the book and kept narrating the town" (Akasaka 1994: 276).

2. "Tônopia"

Tôno City started to show an interest in *Tôno monogatari* from the point of view of regional development in the 1970s. Around that time a key catchphrase in tourism was "Discover Japan." This was a reaction against the disappearance of the old Japan during the period of high-speed economic growth of the 1960s. During this period in Tôno, the *magariya* or traditional houses built in a distinctive regional style gradually disintegrated. Komazawa Nizaeimon who runs *Minshuku Magariya*, a guest house built in the traditional style, recollects them:

> At that time the old things were rapidly being demolished. I felt a tinge of sadness about this, and wondered whether things which were rooted in the locality might not be useful in some way. The traditional houses are perhaps something that the old people can regard with nostalgia, and the younger people can regard as curious.

At the same time, the works of Yanagita were widely read by young people, including *Tôno monogatari*, and a "Yanagita boom" began. Furthermore, a project called "Tônopia" was planned in Tôno, and the idea of the "rural museum city" became a key concept in the development of the region. The Tônopia plan fitted well with the Ohira cabinet's ideas of giving priority to the regions (*chihô*) and the creation of garden cities, and it also fitted nicely with the government's plan to promote development that would harmonize the interests of the rural areas and the cities.

Figure 11.2. Tôno: Local products on display at
Mukashibanashi Village.

The thinking which underlay the Tônopia plan was as follows. From the
period of the Meiji "enlightenment" onwards, Japan started to import the
Western system, including its academic disciplines. Japanese folklore studies, however, is noteworthy as one of the few exceptions, and it became a
discipline because of *Tôno monogatari*, making Tôno the birthplace of Japanese folklore studies. As a result, Tôno is a mecca for research into myth,
and a place that the Japanese consider a generalized *furusato* or homeland.[4]
Accordingly, Tôno City labeled itself *minwa no furusato* (the home of folk
tales) and made folk tales the basis of its tourist development policy. To implement the policy, a Tôno City Museum, a Tôno Folklore Village (Tôno
Mukashibanashi Mura), and a Heritage Park (Denshôen) were established in
the 1980s. The City Museum was established in 1980, and it displays the
traditional village world of Tôno, divided into three sections. The first part is
the "World of the *Tôno monogatari*" in which people can enjoy watching
films about this world on multiple screens. The second is "Tôno's Natural
World and Way of Life," which is an exhibition of items such as those used
in agriculture and festivals. The third section explains the city's folklore. The
original manuscript of the *Tôno monogatari* is on display, and visitors can
see a video of the culture of everyday life in Tôno.

Tôno Folklore Village or Tôno Mukashibanashi Mura was established in
1985. ("Mukashibanashi" in Japanese corresponds to the phrase "Once upon

Figure 11.3. Tôno: Folktale recitation at Mukashibanashi Village.

a time" in English.) It consists of a cluster of houses, but the most important is a building called the Ryûôjuku. This is where the guest house, Takazen Ryokan, in which Yanagita stayed when he visited the town in 1908, has been relocated and renamed. Next to this is the *Monogatari Kura* (treasury of stories), and the *Utage no Kura* (a banquet hall). At the back is Yanagita's study, which has also been relocated, from Tokyo. In addition, recitations of Tôno folk tales by local storytellers can be heard in the Mukashibanashi Hall on the second floor of the souvenir shop. When I visited it in 1994, folk tales in the Tôno dialect were being performed in rotation by six people, including Suzuki Satsu (b. 1911), each recitation lasting up to 30 minutes. The tourists listening to the tales said that they experienced a sense of simplicity (*soboku*) and nostalgia (*natsukashisa*), and that it was interesting to hear about a world of which they knew nothing. According to the manager of the Folklore Village, Taniguchi Tetsutaro, since outsiders became interested in the folk tales, the local people have recently started to accept them as well.

Heritage Park or Denshôen is only 15 minutes by car away from Tôno, at Dobuchi, the birthplace of Sasaki Kizen. Here, some farm houses in the distinctive local style, *nambu magariya*, have been moved and rebuilt, and the aim is to reconstruct Tôno village life. According to the manager, Tanichi Nobuo, the local old people's association played an important role in this.

For instance, the old people are reviving annual customs such as *mushioi* (driving away the insects), involving the local children, thus maintaining tradition in the guise of social education. The old people of the region are also making local handicrafts and selling them as souvenirs. This is a business that makes use of the old people's knowledge and abilities, and not just a case of them helping out. In January of each year, at the winter event called "Tônopia" (the Tôno folklore festival), folk tales are told around the *irori*, the sunken hearths of the traditional houses. There are a number of tourist sites dotted around the town, including Torii, the site of the old Hayachine pilgrims' road; Kappabuchi, the *kappa* pool, famous from the tales; the traditional house of the Chiba family; and the Yamaguchi water wheel.

In 1992, a world folklore exhibition was held at Tôno. The aim was to transmit information on folklore from Tôno, the "home of folklore," to the rest of the world (Tôno City 1994: 25). In the first edition of *Tôno monogatari*, Yanagita actually dedicated the book to "the people of foreign countries." Participants came from thirteen countries in all, including Russia, Bulgaria, Mexico, India, Malaysia, China, and Korea. Seminars were held on the folklore of *oni* (goblins) and "urban folklore and the future of the world," and performances included music from dance rituals in other parts of the world. The stage used at this event is now used for the recitation of folk tales just mentioned.

In 1994, about 400,000 tourists visited Tôno, which is not a particularly large number for a Japanese tourist site. But the Tônopia project has not yet been fully realized, and the plan is still underway. It has three basic themes: "a city full of space, light and greenery," "a city of health with culture, rich in humanity," and a "city which is a museum park for nature, history, and folklore" (Tôno City 1992: 2-3). The last of these provides the unique element in the plan. Tôno City was established in 1954 by the unification of seven previously separate villages. These former villages are in the process of setting up local centers and public halls as a focus for the revival of their distinctive characteristics. The aim is the creation of a "museum park city" bringing together these three elements of nature, history, and local culture. As Matsuzaki Kenzô shows, this concept is similar to that of the "ecomuseum" (Matsuzaki 1990: 315-16). In other words, the aim is to promote the region by preserving, encouraging, and presenting the living environment in its original location, including nature, society, and culture. To relate this directly to tourism, tourism in Tôno could become significant as an example of ecotourism in this wider sense.

143

3. Re-appropriating Tôno

In anthropology, the phenomenon of tourism has often been dealt with within the framework of "acculturation" in which a weaker culture is absorbed by a stronger one. On the other hand, Ôta has discussed tourism in terms of the politically weak hosts reversing the unequal power relations between hosts and tourists, and negotiating and constructing their own identity (Ôta 1993 1998: 71). From this perspective the following points are important for Tôno. As I have suggested previously, the Tôno project is an attempt to re-appropriate for the Tôno region itself something that Yanagita formerly appropriated for metropolitan Japan. Miyoshi Kyozô gives a frank description of the ambivalent feelings that Sasaki Kizen, who came from the area, had towards Yanagita who was at that time a government official (Miyoshi 1991). According to Kikuchi Takeshi, a high school teacher in social studies, "Tôno's history is one of longing for the 'center,' i.e. Tokyo, and then being exploited, cheated and eventually ripped off by it." As a depopulated city, Tôno is seen by the older people who remain there as having been continually deprived of its young people by the metropolis.

Against this background, the activities of the Tôno Jômin Daigaku (Tôno Folk University) are significant: it holds meetings in various places throughout the country, organized by Gotoh Sôichiro who is carrying out research on Yanagita from the point of view of the history of ideas. This series of meetings began in 1986, and the thirteenth meeting was held in Tôno in 1994. The chairman of the management committee, Koiguchi Tamotsu, is a person who once migrated to Tokyo, but then returned to Tôno. He says that unless the provincial regions become stronger through study, an "age of the regions" will be impossible. One piece of original research by the university is a commentary on *Tôno monogatari* that the Tôno people themselves have been preparing for ten years; and committee member Takayanagi Toshio has been retracing the route by which Yanagita came to Tôno.[5]

Concerning the relationship between research on *Tôno monogatari* and tourism, Koiguchi points out: "If you study *Tôno monogatari* as a commodity, the way in which this has to be marketed is rather different. This means that the Folk University's activities must be related to tourism. If you trace the tales back to their origins, a broader kind of tourism is perhaps possible." In this project the Tôno tourist industry does not simply follow Yanagita's book: it is also clear that the local people are attempting to create their own tourism based on their own folk tales.

4. The creation of a regional culture

What must once more be stressed is Hobsbawm's point, that in many cases tradition is a recent "invention" (Hobsbawm and Ranger 1983) – or, following Jocelyn Linnekin, a "reconstruction" (Linnekin 1992). Many people may object to the idea of tradition being "invented," but as Sanjek says, culture is always on the move, and is subject to "continuous creation" (Sanjek 1991: 622). So-called pristine "ethnic" or "traditional cultures" are no more than fabrications. As I said in chapter 1, when we think about today's ethnic and traditional cultures, what we have to accept is that our viewpoint should not be one of "narratives of loss" linked to theories of acculturation, but rather "narratives of emergence" linked to theories of cultural dynamics.

The following account from a teacher at Tôno Primary School, Arata Michiko, is worth noting here. A folklore festival was planned at the school in 1992, and the children were given an assignment to listen to folk tales at home, with the aim of collecting them together. However, the results were not very good, as even the children's grandparents did not know any stories. The result was that the children had to go to the Tôno City Museum and the Denshôen to hear the stories. Significantly, these institutions, which were set up for tourists, are also playing a role for the local people. With a little reflection it seems obvious that folk tales are not transmitted naturally even in the "home of folklore," but that a conscious attempt has to be made to recreate them. At Tôno Primary School, the children put on performances of folklore based on the Tôno stories, and this serves as a means of cultural transmission. The winter Tônopia, which takes place in January, and the Tôno Mukashibanashi Festival also serve this purpose.

Within this context, the youngest member of the group of narrators, Hosogoe Masako (b. 1954) gave this account:

> [In the transmission of folklore] first of all the dialect itself is changing. It would not have happened in the days before television and radio, but the Tôno dialect itself will probably disappear in the next twenty or thirty years. We cannot pass on Tôno as it is: the only thing that we can do to some extent is to pass on something that *simulates* Tôno [*Tônorashisa*].

The point here is that in this conscious process of transmission the substance of the local culture is itself changing. As with ethnicity, substantive changes in culture arise in an intercultural context in which specific cultural elements are selected and taken up. Although the cultures of present-day Bali and Tôno are only hybrid entities, they give rise to statements such as "*kecak* is the soul of Balinese culture" or "*Tôno monogatari* is the real essence of Tôno." However, as Hosogoe says, cultural transmission is probably only the recreation of a similar style or a likeness (*rashisa*).

This likeness is, on the one hand, the essence of a culture, but, at the same time, it is also a copy. The tourist cultural show or souvenir artifacts are typical examples of this. In Tôno, cassette tapes made by the folk tale narrators are sold as souvenirs, and in Bali they sell cassettes of *kecak* and gamelan music. What is significant is that these things are bought not only by tourists. Hosogoe says that she learned folk tales through these tapes, and in Bali they are also used in dance rehearsals. In addition, among the Balinese who have migrated to Jakarta and elsewhere, listening to these tapes is becoming a way of confirming self-identity. Cultural transmission is thus a complex process of copying and recreation.

Notes

1. The work has been translated into English by Ronald Morse as *The Legends of Tôno* (Tokyo: Japan Foundation, 1975); and by Toda Shizuo as *Tôno monogatari: Folklore and Tradition in the Tôno Districts* (Sendai: Shohan, 1983).

2. The interview material from this chapter is drawn from the videos produced by the National Museum of Japanese History at Sakura, *Kankô to minzoku bunka: Tôno minzokushi 1994/95* (Tourism and Folk Culture: Tôno 1994/95), and *Minzoku bunka jiki hyôgen: Tôno Minzokushi 1994/95* (Folk Culture and Self Representation: Tôno 1994/95). These videos were edited by Kawamori Hiroshi (1995a, b). I participated in the project in July-August 1994 and January 1995.

3. As Iwamoto (1983: 12) points out, this kind of image may sometimes be problematic for the people of Tôno, because it reinforces the stereotype held by visitors from cities. As Iwamoto writes, it is unreasonable to visit Tôno in the expectation of encounters with the supernatural, and in the belief that imaginary creatures live in the mountains or the rivers, and that the people living in Tôno belong to that world as well. Visitors who think this will be as disappointed as Orikuchi Shinobu when he went there for the first time in late August, 1930. He was dismayed to find that Tôno was already different from what was described in *Tôno monogatari*, and he envied his master, Yanagita Kunio, who had been able to experi-

ence the "authentic" landscapes of Tôno, which Orikuchi thought that he had come too late to see.

4. Tôno-shi, "Tônopia puran III: shizen to rekishi to minzoku no hakubutsukoen toshi kensetsu kôsô," (Tônopia plan, III: Constructing a Museum Park City of Nature, History, and Folklore), p. 6. A direct translation of the relevant passage in the original brochure is given by Ivy (1995: 114).

5. This was published in 1997 in a book edited by the Tôno Jômin Daigaku.

Chapter 12

Between the Global and the Local:

Learning from the Anthropology of Tourism

This is the age of globalization and disappearing boundaries. In this last chapter, I summarize the argument so far, and suggest that thinking of globalization and localization, or modernity and tradition as being opposed to each other is actually incorrect. My own view is that what cultural anthropology today should illuminate is the realm which lies between the global and the local. The anthropology of tourism presents us with a challenge to do just this.

1. Tourism and the globalization of culture

In this book, I have described various aspects of the cultural dynamism of today's world of globalization and disappearing boundaries, using tourism as a way of looking at the problem. The main setting has been Bali in Indonesia, but I have also discussed the additional cases of the Toraja in Indonesia, the Sepik River region of Papua New Guinea, and Tôno in Japan. Through these examples, I have tried to show that tourism is not just a commercial activity, but rather that it is also closely linked to the production of culture in the contemporary world. In conclusion I should probably also say something about the relationship between the global and the local, which is important in thinking about contemporary culture. On the one hand, tourism is linked to global migration, but, at the same time, it is also linked to cultural localization.

Generally speaking, is the world becoming more homogeneous along with the process of globalization, and are the global and the local really opposed to each other? In thinking about these questions, I want to consider the concept of "glocalization" suggested by the sociologist, Roland Robertson:

According to *The Oxford Dictionary of New Words* (1991: 134) the term "glocal" is "formed by telescoping global and local to make a blend." Also according to the Dictionary that idea has been "modelled on Japanese dochakuka (deriving from dochaku, "living on one's own land"), originally the agricultural principle of adapting one's farming techniques to local conditions, but also adopted in Japanese business for *global localization*, a global outlook adapted to local conditions. (Robertson 1995: 28, emphasis in original.)

In the term "globalization" the image of the world becomes more homogeneous, and thus globalization and localization seem to be in conflict with each other. However, in thinking about globalization there is a recognition that these two terms simply represent two aspects of a single process. From this point of view, the two processes of "ethnic and cultural fragmentation and modernist homogenization" are, as Jonathan Friedman discussed, "not two arguments, two opposing views of what is happening in the world today, but two constitutive trends of global reality" (Friedman 1990: 311).

Seeing things in this way, will the uniqueness of a region be lost as globalization progresses, or will regions at the same time resist globalization and assert themselves? There is no single answer. Rather, regionalism can be thought of as arising only within the global context. While this may be true, as Stuart Hall emphasizes, globalization happens not so much through ironing out the differences as through allowing in differences (Hall 1996). As a result, consciousness of difference is probably accentuated. The tourism discussed in this volume provides insights into both "glocalism" and the globalization that comes through differentiation. So along with globalization, regional culture on the one hand is fragmented, but, on the other hand, local distinctiveness is reconstructed within the context of tourism. By carrying out research on the contact zone between the global system of world capitalism and the local system of the host society that develops through tourism, the ethnography of tourism contributes to dynamic area studies research into the creation of regional culture.

2. The politics of identity

In relation to the influence of tourism on regional society, there are many negative accounts, in contrast to those that stress the economic effects. As was mentioned previously, based on his research on the Basque region, David Greenwood argues angrily that culture has become a commodity and is being sold off, and that as a result the local people sustain a considerable cultural and social loss (Greenwood 1989).[1] The Japanese journalist Matsui Yayori accuses the development of tourism in Asia of not helping the local people, and hastening social and environmental collapse (Matsui 1993). However, it is insufficient just to criticize tourism for bringing about these serious negative changes. Nor is it true that the development of tourism is the only factor giving rise to cultural and social change and environmental collapse. As I have shown in this book, "narratives of loss" regarding traditional culture due to tourist development mistakenly idealize traditional culture as a causal reality, which has been handed down from ancient times. As historians like Hobsbawm have shown, tradition is in many cases a recent invention. A theoretical model of traditional culture changing under the influence of modern civilization cannot explain the dynamism of culture.

In addition there is the existence of culture created by tourism, or "touristic culture." Cultural shows put on for the tourists and souvenir artifacts are typical examples: they are copies and tend to be thought of as having lost their original nature. But tourism rather makes use of (or diverts) traditional culture – whether it be Balinese performance, Toraja ritual, Sepik carving, or Tôno folklore – while influencing the creation of new culture. It is necessary to view things from the perspective of a "narrative of emergence" in order to grasp this process. In this relationship between tourism and the creation of culture, it is a mistake to give an account of tradition and modernity as being opposed to each other. As with the example of Indonesian batik discussed by Sekimoto Teruo, tradition is not something of the past, but rather of the present, and this is highly significant. Tradition is always something that we experience today (Sekimoto 2003).

Within this context, tourism becomes an excellent site for the study of identity. As was seen in the quotation from Picard in chapter 4, tourism did not lead either to the breakdown of Balinese culture or, on the contrary, to its preservation, but created a consciousness among the Balinese of their own culture (Picard 1995: 60). Marie-Françoise Lanfant, in the introduction to a book she edited on international tourism, wrote: "As is often said, we carry out research on the social and cultural impact of tourism. In other words we try to deal with its external impact, and to establish in what ways they are positive or negative, and we have followed this single line of research" (Lanfant et al. 1995: 1). Significantly, in the case of Bali discussed in this book, along with Toraja, the Sepik River, and Tôno, tourism does not simply consist of staging the local culture for the tourists: it is also the arena in which negotiations concerning cultural identity take place. This means that in the context of tourism, culture clearly reflects the dynamism of the oscillation between globalization and localization, image and reality, substance and copy, subjectivity and objectivity, and it is closely linked with the practice of their own culture by the local people.

3. The implications of the anthropology of tourism

In reviewing research in the anthropology of tourism, Malcolm Crick argues:

> Anthropology has often been defined as the study of human beings in culture and society. Tourism is thus an odd anthropological object, because international tourists are people out of culture in at least two senses. First, they do not belong to the culture of the destination country, and second, they have stepped beyond the bounds of ordinary social reality into what has sometimes been referred to as a "ludic" or "liminoid" realm. (Crick 1989: 332)

The lifestyle of international tourism, which involves living a double existence – inside and outside culture and society, as well as both work and leisure – means that people are separated from their home areas and move across international boundaries. If we look at the present from a place within what Appadurai (1990) calls "global cultural flows," this becomes more and more striking.

Tourism, rather than being an eccentric object of study for anthropologists, is, on the contrary, essential if anthropologists are to restructure the objects of their research. Anthropologists formerly used to assume that, in a given area, a given people live with a given culture. This kind of static ethnological and anthropological viewpoint cannot deal with the "realm in between." The new kind of anthropology, which extends to migratory lifestyles, must be shaped in the gaps between cultures and between societies. The anthropology of tourism presents one challenging attempt to do just this.

Note

1. Greenwood's paper was first published in 1977, and republished in 1989. In the 1989 version the author added that it was necessary to rethink his indignation in the wider context of large-scale cultural change (1989: 181-85).

Bibliography

Acciaioli, Greg. 1985. "Culture as art: From practice to spectacle in Indonesia," *Canberra Anthropology* 8: 148-72.

Adams, Kathleen. 1984. "Come to Tana Toraja, 'Land of Heavenly Kings': Travel agents as brokers in ethnicity," *Annals of Tourism Research* 11: 469-85.

Ahmed, Akbar and Cris Shore eds. 1995. *The Future of Anthropology: Its Relevance to the Contemporary World*. London and Atlantic Highlands, NJ: Athlone.

Akasaka Norio. 1994. *Tôno/Monogatarikô* [Tôno and its tales]. Tokyo: Takarajimasha.

Anderson, Benedict. 1992. "The new world disorder," *New Left Review* 193 (May/June).

Appadurai, Arjun.1990. "Disjuncture and difference in the global cultural economy," pp. 295-310 in *Global Culture: Nationalism, Globalization and Modernity*, ed. Mike Featherstone. London: Sage Publications.

Appadurai, Arjun. 1991. "Global ethnoscapes: Notes and queries for a transnational anthropology," pp. 191-210 in *Recapturing Anthropology*, ed. Richard Fox. Santa Fe: School of American Research Press.

Atkinson, Jane Monnig. 1983. "Religions in dialogue: The construction of Indonesian minority religion," *American Ethnologist* 10: 684-96.

Aziz, Arnicun ed. 1994. *Lima GBHN 1973-1993*. Jakarta: Sinar Grafika.

Bagus, I Gusti Ngrah. 1992. "Kebangkitan, Arah Reformasi dan Masa Depan," pp. 51-69 in *Hindu Bicara*, Putu Setia ed. Jakarta: Yayasan Dharma Naradha.

Bandem, I Made. 1995. "Profil Seni Masa Depan," pp. 113.-126 in *Bali di Persimpangan Jalan 1.* Usadi Wiryatnaya and Jean Couteau eds. Denpasar: Nusa Data Indo Budaya.

Bandem, I Made and Fredrik Eugene deBoer. 1981. *Kaja and Kelod: Balinese Dance in Transition.* Kuala Lumpur: Oxford University Press.

Bateson, Gregory and Margaret Mead. 1942. *Balinese Character: A Photographic Analysis.* New York: The New York Academy of Sciences.

Baudrillard, Jean. 1981. *Simulacres et simulation.* Paris: Galilee.

Belo, Jane. 1970. *Traditional Balinese Culture.* New York and London: Columbia University Press.

Ben-Amos, Paula. 1977. "Pidgin languages and tourist arts," *Studies in the Anthropology of Visual Communication* 4 (2): 128-39.

Bloch, Maurice. 1986. *From Blessing to Violence.* Cambridge: Cambridge University Press.

Boon, James A. 1979. "Balinese temple politics and the religious revitalization of caste ideals," pp. 271-91 in *The Imagination of Reality: Essays in Southeast Asian Coherence Systems.* A. L. Becker and A. A. Yengoyan eds. Norwood, NJ: ABLEX.

Boon, James A. 1986. "Between-the-war Bali: Rereading the relics," pp. 218-47 in *Malinowski, Rivers, Benedict and Others: Essays on Culture and Personality.* G.W. Stocking Jr. ed. Seattle: The University of Washington Press.

Boorstin, Daniel. 1963. *The Image, or, What Happened to the American Dream.* Harmondsworth, Middlesex: Pelican.

Bourdieu, Pierre. 1977. *Outline of a Theory of Practice.* Cambridge: Cambridge University Press.

Bourdieu, Pierre. 1984. *Distinction: A Social Critique of the Judgement of Taste.* Cambridge, Massachusetts: Harvard University Press.

Bruner, Edward M. 1989. "Of cannibals, tourists, and ethnographers," *Cultural Anthropology* 4: 438-45.

Bruner, Edward M. 1995. "The ethnographer/tourist in Indonesia," pp. 224-41 in *International Tourism: Identity and Change.* Marie-Françoise Lanfant, John B. Allcock and Edward M. Bruner eds. London: Sage Publications.

Chaplin, Charles. 1964. *My Autobiography.* London: The Bodley Head.

Clifford, James. 1988. *The Predicament of Culture: Twentieth-Century Ethnography, Literature, and Art.* Cambridge and London: Harvard University Press.

Clifford, James. 1992. "Traveling cultures," pp. 96-116 in *Cultural Studies.*

L. Grossberg, C. Nelson and P. Treichler eds. New York: Routledge.

Clifford, James. 1997. *Routes: Travel and Translation in the Late Twentieth Century*. Cambridge, Mass. and London: Harvard University Press.

Cohen, Erik. 1979. "A phenomenology of tourist experiences," *Sociology* 13: 179-201.

Covarrubias, Miguel. 1937. *Island of Bali*. New York: A.A. Knopf.

Crick, Malcolm. 1989 "Representations of international tourism in the social sciences: Sun, sex, sights, savings and servility," *Annual Review of Anthropology* 18: 307-44.

de Kadt, Emanuel.1992. "Making the alternative sustainable: Lessons from development for tourism," pp. 47-75 in *Tourism Alternatives*. V. Smith and W.R. Eadington eds. Philadelphia: The University of Pennsylvania Press.

Featherstone, Mike ed. 1990. *Global Culture: Nationalism, Globalization and Modernity*. London: Sage Publcations.

Featherstone, Mike, Scott Lash and Roland Robertson eds. 1995. *Global Modernities*. London: Sage Publications.

Feifer, Maxine. 1985. *Going Places: The Ways of the Tourist from Imperial Rome to the Present Day*. London: Macmillan.

Forge, Anthony. 1981. "Balinese religion and Indonesian identity," pp. 221-33 in *Indonesia: The Making of a Culture*. James Fox ed. Canberra: Research School of Pacific Studies, The Australian National University.

Friedman, Jonathan. 1990. "Being in the world: Globalization and localization," pp. 311-28 in *Global Culture: Nationalism, Globalization and Modernity*. Mike Featherstone ed. London: Sage Publications.

Fuke Yosuke. 1991. "Kankô sangyô" [The tourist industry], pp. 122-23 in *Indoneshia no Jiten* [Encyclopedia of Indonesia]. Kyoto: Dôhôsha.

Fukushima Masato. 1991. "Shinkô" no tanjô: Indoneshia ni okeru mainaa shûkyô no tôsô" [The birth of "belief": The struggle of minor religions in contemporary Indonesia], *Tôyô Bunka Kenkyûsho Kiyô* [Memoirs of the Institute of Oriental Studies, University of Tokyo] 113: 97-210.

Geertz, Clifford. 1973. *The Intepretation of Cultures*. New York: Basic Books.

Geertz, Clifford. 1980. *Negara: The Theatre State in Nineteenth-Century Bali*. Princeton, NJ: Princeton University Press.

Geertz, Clifford. 1983. *Local Knowledge*. New York: Basic Books.

Geriya, I Wayan. 1996. "Tourism impact, cultural resistance and patterns of local community's participation response: An anthropological study on the process of Balinization and globalization in three villages of tourism object in Bali." Paper presented at the Japan-Southeast Asia Workshop.

October 31-November 1, Tokyo.

Gewertz, Deborah B. and Frederick K. Errington. 1991. *Twisted Histories, Altered Contexts: Representing the Chamberi in a World System*. Cambridge: Cambridge University Press.

Gorer, Geoffrey. 1987 [1936]. *Bali and Angkor: A 1930s Pleasure Trip Looking at Life and Death*. Singapore: Oxford University Press.

Graburn, Nelson. 1989. "Tourism: The sacred journey, " pp. 21-36 in *Hosts and Guests: The Anthropology of Tourism*. Valene Smith ed. Philadelphia: The University of Pennsylvania Press (second edition).

Graburn, Nelson. 1995. "Tourism, modernity and nostalgia," pp. 158-78 in *The Future of Anthropology: Its Relevance to the Contemporary World*. Akbar Ahmed and Cris Shore eds. London and Atlantic Highlands, NJ: Athlone.

Greenwood, Davydd. 1989. "Culture by the pound: An anthropological perspective on tourism as cultural commoditization," pp. 171-185 in *Hosts and Guests: The Anthropology of Tourism*. Valene L. Smith ed. Philadelphia: The University of Pennsylvania Press (second edition).

Hall, Stuart. 1996. "The dialogue with cultural studies," Lecture given at the University of Tokyo, March 15, 1996.

Hanna, A. Willard. 1990. *Bali Profile: People, Events, Circumstances (1001-1976)*. Moluccas, East Indonesia: Rumah Budaya Naira.

Hannerz, Ulf. 1989. "Culture between center and periphery: Toward a macroanthropology," *Ethnos* 54: 200-16.

Hannerz, Ulf. 1992. *Cultural Complexity: Studies in the Social Organization of Meaning*. New York: Colombia University Press.

Hichcock, Michael, Victor. T. King and Michael. J. G. Parnwell eds. 1993. *Tourism in South-East Asia*. London and New York: Routledge.

Hisada Megumi. 1992. *Firipiina wo ai shita otokotachi* [The men who loved Filipinas]. Tokyo: Bungei Shunjusha.

Hobsbawm, Eric and Terence Ranger eds. 1983. *The Invention of Tradition*. Cambridge: Cambridge University Press.

Honjo Yasuhisa. 1996. *Tômasu Kukku no tabi: Kindai tsûrisumu no tanjô* [Thomas Cook's tours: The birth of modern tourism]. Tokyo: Kôdansha.

Ieda Shoko. 1991. *Ierô kabu: Narita wo tobi satta onnatachi* [The yellow cab: Women who flew from Narita]. Tokyo: Kôyû Shuppan.

Imafuku Ryuta. 1991. *Kureôru shugi* [Creolism]. Tokyo: Seidosha.

Inose Kumiko. 1990. *Daiei teikoku wa myûshikku hôru kara* [The British Empire seen from the music hall]. Tokyo: Asahi Shinbunsha.

Ishimori Shûzô. 1990. "Kokusai kankô akademi: Kankô kenkyû no saikin no dôkô" [The International Academy for the Study of Tourism: Recent directions in tourism research], *Minpaku Tsûshin* [Newsletter of the National Museum of Ethnology] 47: 70-86.

Ivy, Marilyn. 1995. *Discourses of the Vanishing: Modernity, Phantasm, Japan.* Chicago: The University of Chicago Press.

Iwamoto Yoshiteru. 1983. *Mo hitotsu no "Tôno monogatari"* [Alternative "Tales of Tôno"). Tokyo: Toshui Shobô.

Jameson, Fredric. 1983. "Postmodernism and consumer society," pp. 111-25 in *Postmodern Culture.* Hal Foster ed. London: Pluto Press.

Kagami Haruya. 1992. "Jakaruta no Barijin" [Hindu-Balinese in Jakarta], *Tônan Ajia Kenkyû* [Southeast Asian Research] 30: 315-330.

Kagami Haruya. 1995. "Girei no seisô rongi ni miru Bari no shûkyô jijô" [Invention of religion and customs in contemporary Bali], *Minzokugaku Kenkyû* [The Japanese Journal of Ethnology] 60: 32-52.

Kagami Haruya. 1997. "Okushidentarizumu" [Occidentalism], pp. 59-83 in *Iwanami kôza bunkajinruigaku 8: Ibunka no kyôzai* [Iwanami Series in Cultural Anthropology, vol. 8, The coexistence of different cultures]. Tokyo: Iwanami Shoten.

Kammerer, Cornelia Ann. 1990. "Custom and Christian conversion among Akha Highlanders of Burma and Thailand," *American Ethnologist* 17: 277-91.

Karatani Kôjin. 1988. *Kindai Nihon bungaku no kigen* [The origins of modern Japanese literature]. Tokyo: Kodansha.

Kawamori Hiroshi. 1995a. *Kankô to minzoku bunka: Tôno minzokushi 94/ 95* [Tourism and folk culture: The ethnography of Tono, 94/95]. Sakura: National Museum of Japanese History (video).

Kawamori Hiroshi. 1995b. *Minzoku bunka no jiko hyôgen: Tôno minzokushi 94/95* [How folk ethnic culture expresses itself: The ethnography of Tono, 94/95]. Sakura: The National Museum of Japanese History (video).

Kawamori Hiroshi. 1996. "Nosutarujia to dentô bunka no saikôsei: Tôno no minhua kankô" [Nostalgia and the rebirth of traditional culture: Folktale tourism in Tôno], pp. 150-58 in *Kankô jinruigaku* [The anthropology of tourism]. Yamashita Shinji ed. Tokyo: Shinyôsha.

Kelsky, Karen. 1996. "Flirting with the foreign: International sex in Japan's 'international' age," pp. 173-92 in *Global/Local.* Rob Wilson and Wimal Dissanayake eds. Durham and London: Duke University Press.

Kelsky, Karen. 1999. "Gender, modernity and eroticized internationalism in Japan," *Cultural Anthropology* 14: 229-55.

Kida Midori. 1998. *Onnatachiyo, Amerika e itte dô suru no?* [Ladies, what are you going to do in America?). Tokyo: PHP Kenkyûsho.

Kipp, Rita and Susan Rodgers eds. 1987. *Indonesian Religions in Transition*. Tucson: The University of Arizona Press.

Koke, Louise G. 1987. *Our Hotel in Bali*. Wellington: January Books.

Krause, Gregor. 1922. *Insel Bali*. Hagen i. W.: Folkwang-Verlag GMBH. (English version, published in 1988 as *Bali 1912*. Wellington: January Books).

Kruhse-Mount Burton, Suzy. 1995. "Sex tourism and traditional Australian male identity," pp. 192-204 in *International Tourism: Identity and Change*. Marie-Françoise Lanfant, J. B. Allcock and E. Bruner eds. London: Sage Publications.

Lanfant, Marie-Françoise, J.B. Allcock and E. Bruner eds. 1995. *International Tourism: Identity and Change*. London: Sage Publications.

Leach, Edmund. 1961. *Rethinking Anthropology*. London: Athlone.

Linnekin, Jocelyn. 1992. "On the theory and politics of cultural construction in the Pacific," *Oceania* 62: 249-63.

Lyon, M. L. 1980. "The Hindu revival in Java: Politics and religious identity, " pp. 205-19 in *Indonesia: The Making of a Culture*. James Fox ed. Canberra: Research School of Pacific Studies, The Australian National University.

MacCannell, Dean. 1973. "Staged authenticity: Arrangements of social space in tourist settings," *American Journal of Sociology* 79: 589-603.

MacCannell, Dean. 1976. *The Tourist: A New Theory of the Leisure Class*. New York: Schocken Books.

MacCannell, Dean. 1992. *Empty Meeting Grounds: The Tourist Papers*. London and New York: Routledge.

Maekawa Kenichi. 1989. *Kaisetsu: Pôru Gôgan Noa Noa: Tahichi kikô* [Commentary: Noa Noa: the travel dairy of Paul Gauguin]. Tokyo: Iwanami Shoten.

Matsuda, Misa. 1989. Japanese Tourists and Indonesia: Images of Self and Other in the Age of *Kokusaika* (Internationalization). MA Thesis. Asian Studies, The Australian National University.

Matsui Yayaori. 1993. *Ajia no kankô to Nihon* [Japan and the development of tourism in Asia]. Tokyo: Shinkansha.

Matsuzaka Kenzou. 1990. "Kasochiiki no kasseika" [The revitalization of depopulated regions], pp. 305-30 *in Shôwaki sanson no minzoku bunka* [The folk culture of mountain villages in the Shôwa period]. Seijô Daigaku Minzokugaku Kenkyûjo [Institute for Folklore Studies, Seijô University], ed. Tokyo: Meichô Shuppan.

157

Maurer, Jean-Luc. 1979. *Tourism and Development in a Socio-economic Perspective: Indonesia as a Case Study.* Geneva: Institut Universitaire des Etudes du Développement.

McKean, Philip. 1973. Cultural Involution: Tourists, Balinese, and the Process of Modernization in an Anthropological Perspective. Ph.D.Dissertation, Brown University.

McKean, Philip. 1989. "Toward a theoretical analysis of tourism: Economic dualism and cultural involution in Bali," pp. 93-108 in *Hosts and Guests: The Anthropology of Tourism.* Valene Smith ed. Philadelphia: The University of Pennsylvania Press (second edition).

McPhee, Colin. 1947. *A House in Bali.* London: Gollancz.

Mead, Margaret. 1972. *Blackberry Winter: My Earlier Years.* New York: Simon & Schuster.

Mead, Margaret. 1977. *Letters from the Field, 1925-1975.* New York: Harper & Row.

Miyauchi Katsusuke. 1995. *Baritô no hibi* [Days in the island of Bali]. Tokyo: Shûeisha.

Miyoshi Kyouzo. 1991. *Tôno yume shijin: Sasaki Kizen to Yanagita Kunio* [The poet of Tôno fantasy: Sasaki Kizen and Yanagita Kunio]. Tokyo: PHP Kenkyûsho.

Moeran, Brian. 1983. "The language of Japanese tourism," *Annals of Tourism Research* 10: 93-108.

Moon, Okpyo. 1998. "Tourism and cultural development: Japanese and Korean contexts," pp. 178-93 in *Tourism and Cultural Development in Asia and Oceania.* Shinji Yamashita, Kadir H. Din and J.S. Eades eds. Bangi, Malaysia: Penerbit Universiti Kebangsaan Malaysia.

Nagafuchi Yasuyuki. 1994. "1917 nen Bari daijishin: Shokuminchi jôkyô ni okeru bunka keisei no seijigaku" [The great Bali earthquake of 1917: The politics of cultural creation during the colonial period], *Kokuritsu Minzokugaku Hakubutsukan Kenkyû Hôkoku* [The Bulletin of the National Museum of Ethnology] 19: 259-310.

Nagafuchi Yasuyuki. 1996. "Kankô = shokuminchishugi no takurami" [Tourism = colonialist plot], pp. 35-44 in *Kankô jinruigaku* [The anthropology of tourism]. Yamashita Shinji ed. Tokyo: Shinyôsha.

Nagafuchi Yasuyuki. 1997. "Bunkateki keni no rekishika to sono kaiji: Bari ni okeru Hindû, hô, kâsuto" [Uncovering cultural authority: Hinduism, law and caste in Balinese modern history], pp. 214-40 in *Shokuminchi shugi to bunka: Jinruigaku no pâspekutiv* [Colonialism and culture: An anthropological perspective]. Yamashita Shinji and Yamamoto Matori, eds. Tokyo: Shinyôsha.

Nagafuchi Yasuyuki. 1994. *Baritô* [The Island of Bali]. Tokyo: Kôdansha.

Nakamura Kiyoshi. 1990. "'Barika' ni tsuite" [On "Balinization"], *Shakaijinruigaku Nenpô* [Annals of Social Anthropology] 16: 179-91.

Nash, Dennison. 1995. "Prospects for tourism study in anthropology," pp. 179-202 in *The Future of Anthropology: Its Relevance to the Contemporary World*. Akbar Ahmed and Cris Shore eds. London and Atlantic Highlands, NJ: Athlone.

Nishikawa Nagao. 1992. *Kokyô no koekata* [Transcending national boundaries]. Tokyo: Chikuma Shobô.

Obayashi Taryo. 1984. *Tônan Ajia no minzoku to rekishi* [Peoples and history of Southeast Asia]. Tokyo: Yamakawa Shuppansha.

Oka, Ida Bagus. 1992. "A sub-system of cultural tourism in Bali," pp. 123-31 in *Universal Tourism: Enriching or Degrading Culture?* Wiendu Nuryanti ed.Yogyakarta: Gadjah Mada University Press.

Okamoto Masako. 1996. *Kaihatsu to bunka* [Development and culture]. Tokyo: Iwanami Shoten.

Ôta Yoshinobu. 1993. "Bunka no kyakutaika: Kankô o tôshita bunka to aidentiti no sôzô" [The objectification of culture: The creation of culture and identity in the tourist world], *Minzokugaku Kenkyû* [Japanese Journal of Ethnology] 57: 383-410.

Ôta Yoshinobu. 1998. *Toransupojishon no shisô: Bunkajinruigaku no saisôzô* [The idea of transposition: Reimagining cultural anthropology]. Tokyo: Sekaishisôsha.

Pfafflin, George, F. 1987. "Concern for tourism: European perspective and response," *Annals of Tourism Research* 14, 576-79.

Picard, Michel. 1990. ""Cultural tourism" in Bali: Cultural performances as tourist Attraction," *Indonesia*, 49: 37-74.

Picard, Michel. 1995. "Cultural heritage and tourist capital: Cultural tourism in Bali," pp. 44-66 in *International Tourism: Identity and Change*. Marie-Françoise Lanfant, J.B. Allcock and E. Bruner eds. London: Sage Publications.

Picard, Michel. 1996. *Bali: Cultural Tourism and Tourist Culture*. Singapore: Archipelago Press.

Picard, Michel and Robert E. Wood eds. 1997. *Tourism, Ethnicity and the State in Asian and Pacific Society*. Honolulu: University of Hawaii Press.

Pieterse, Jan Nederveen. 1995. "Globalization as hybridization," pp. 45-68 in *Global Modernities*. Mike Featherston, Scott Lash and Roland Robertson eds. London: Sage Publications.

Pollmann, Tessel. 1990. "Margaret Mead's Balinese: The fitting symbols of the American dream," *Indonesia* 49: 1-35.

Powell, Hickman. 1986 [1930]. *The Last Paradise: An American's "Discovery" of Bali in the 1920s.* Singapore: Oxford University Press.

Pratt, Mary Louise. 1992. *Imperial Eyes: Travel Writing and Transculturation.* London and New York: Routledge.

Rhodius, Hans and John Darling. 1980. *Walter Spies and Balinese Art.* Amsterdam: Terra, Zutphen.

Robertson, Roland. 1995. "Glocalization: Time-space and homogeneity-heterogeneity," pp. 25-44 in *Global Modernities.* Mike Featherstone, Scott Lash and Roland Robertson eds. London: Sage Publications.

Robinson, Geoffrey. 1995. *The Dark Side of Paradise: Political Violence in Bali.* Ithaca: Cornell University Press.

Rosaldo, Renato. 1989. *Culture and Truth: The Remaking of Social Analysis.* Boston: Beacon Press.

Sahlins, Marshall. 1985. *Islands of History.* Chicago: University of Chicago Press.

Said, Edward. 1978. *Orientalism.* New York: Pantheon Books.

Sanger, Annette. 1991. "Sawai ka, wazawaika? Balitô no barong dansu to kankô" [Blessing or blight? The Balinese *barong* dance and tourism], in *Kankô to ongaku* [Tourism and music]. Ishimori Shûzô, ed. Tokyo: Shosekisha. (Original English version published in 1998 as "Blessing or blight? The effect of touristic dance-drama on village life in Singapadu, Bali," in *Come mek me hol' yu han': The Impact of Tourism on Traditional Music.* International Council of Traditional Music, ed. Jamaica: Jamaica Memorial Bank.)

Sanjek, Roger. 1991. "The ethnographic present," *Man* (N.S.) 26: 609-28.

Santosa, Silvio. 1988. *Bali Path Finder.* Ubud, Bali (4th edition.).

Schieffelin, Edward and Robert Crittenden. 1991. *Like People You See in a Dream: First Contact in Six Papuan Societies.* Stanford: Stanford University Press.

Schivelbusch, Wolfgang. 1979. *The Railway Journey: Trains and Travel in the 19th Century.* New York: Urizen Books.

Sekimoto, Teruo. 2003. "Batik as a commodity and a cultural object, " pp. 111-25 in *Globalization in Southeast Asia: Local, National and Transnational Perspectives.* Shinji Yamashita and J.S. Eades, eds. New York: Berghahn.

Setia, Putu ed. 1992. *Cendekiawan Hindu Bicara.* Jakarta: Yayasan Dharma Naradha.

Setia, Putu. 1994. *Putu Setia no Bali annai* [Putu Setia's guide to Bali]. Tokyo: Mokuseisha. (Originally published in 1986 in Indonesian as *Menggugat Bali*. Jakarta: PT Pustaka Grafitipers.)

Shimoju Akioko. 1999. *Yureru 24 sai purasu 5 in NY* [Worried twenty-four-year-olds plus five in New York]. Tokyo: Kôdansha.

Shirahata Yozaburo. 1996. *Ryokô no susume* [Invitation to travel]. Tokyo: Chûôkôronsha.

Shiraishi, Saya. 1997. "Japan's soft power: Doraemon goes overseas," pp. 234-72 in *Network Power: Japan and Asia*. Peter J. Katzenstein and Takashi Shiraishi eds. Ithaca: Cornell University Press.

Smith, Valene L. ed. 1977. *Hosts and Guests: The Anthropology of Tourism*. Philadelphia: The University of Pennsylvania Press (first edition).

Smith, Valene L. ed. 1989. *Hosts and Guests: The Anthropology of Tourism*. Philadelphia: The University of Pennsylvania Press (second edition).

Smith, V. and W. R. Eadington eds. 1992. *Tourism Alternatives*. Philadelphia: The University of Pennsylvania Press.

Soejima Hirohiko. 1996. "Warutâ Supîsu to Bali" [Walter Spies and Bali], *Yuriika* [Eureka] 28: 336-39.

Soejima Hirohiko. 1997. "Girei kara atorakushon e: Tôrizumu no naka no kecha" [From ritual to spectacle: the *kecak* in the context of tourism], *Yuriika* [Eureka] 29: 230-41.

Sontag, Susan. 1979. *On Photography*. Harmondsworth, Middlesex: Penguin Books.

Sôrifu [Prime Minister's Office]. 1995. *Heisei 7 nen ban kankô hakusho* [White Paper on Tourism, 1995]. Tokyo: Ôgurashô Insatsukyoku [Ministry of Finance Printing Office].

Sôrifu [Prime Minister's Office]. 1998. *Heisei 10 nen ban kankô hakusho* [White Paper on Tourism, 1998]. Tokyo: Ôgurashô Insatsukyoku [Ministry of Finance Printing Office].

Sternberger, Dolf. 1955. *Panorama, oder Ansichten vom 19. Jahrhundert*. Hamburg. (English version published as *Panorama of the Nineteenth Century*. New York: Urizen Books, 1977.)

Sugimoto Yoshi. 1993. *Nihonjin o yameru hôhô* [The way to stop the Japanese]. Tokyo: Chikuma Shobô.

Sugriwa, I Gusti Bagus Sudhyatmaka ed. 1991. *Pesta Kesenian Bali*. Denpasar: Cita Budaya.

Swellengrebel, Jan Lodewijk. 1960. "Introduction," pp. 1-76 in *Bali: Studies in Life, Thought and Ritual*. W.F. Wertheim, ed. The Hague and Bandung: W. van Hoeve.

Tanabe Shigeharu. 1993. "Jissen shûkyô no jinruigaku: Jôzabu Bukkyô no sekai" [The anthropology of practical religion: The world of Theravada Buddhism], pp. 3-32 in *Jissen shûkyô no jinruigaku* [The anthropology of practical religion]. Tanabe Shigeharu, ed. Kyoto: Kyoto Daigaku Gakujitsu Shuppankai [Kyoto University Academic Press].

Tantri, K'tut. 1981. *Revolt in Paradise*. Jakarta: Gramedia.

Tokai Harumi, Otake Akiko, and Tomari Shinji eds. 1990. *Odoru shima Bari*. [Bali, the island of dance]. Tokyo: PARCO Shuppan.

Tôno City. 1992. *Tônopia puran* [Tônopia plan]. Tôno: Tôno City Hall.

Tôno City. 1994. *'92 sekai minhua semmon Tôno hôkokusho* [Report on the 1992 World Folklore Festival in Tôno]. Tôno: Tôno City Hall.

Tsuchiya Kenji. 1990. "Nashonarizumu" [Nationalism], pp. 147-72 in *Tônan Ajia no shisô* [Thought in Southeast Asia]. Tsuchiya Kenji, ed. Tokyo: Kôbundô.

Tsuchiya Kenji. 1991. *Karutini no fukei* [The landscape of Kartini]. Tokyo: Mekong.

Tsurumi Yoshiyuki. 1981. *Ajia o shiru tame ni* [Introduction to Asia]. Tokyo: Chikuma Shobô.

Turner, Victor. 1969. *The Ritual Process*. Chicago: Aldine.

Ueno Chizuko. 1996. "Heisei fukyôka no onna to otoko" [Men and women in the Heisei recession], *Gekkan Minpaku*, June: 2-7.

Universitas Gadjah Mada. 1992. *Penyusunan Tata Ruang dan Rencana Detail Teknis Desa Wisata Terpadu di Bali. Laporan Terakhir*. Yogyakarta: Fakultas Teknis, Universitas Gadjah Mada.

Universitas Gadjah Mada. 1994. *Penyusunan Rencana Pengbangunan Desa Wisata di Bali. Laporan Terakhir.* Yogyakarta: Fakultas Teknis, Universitas Gadjah Mada.

Urry, John. 1990. *The Tourist Gaze*. London: Sage.

Vickers, Adrian. 1989. *Bali: A Paradise Created.* Berkeley and Singapore: Periplus Editions.

Volkman, Toby Alice. 1990. "Visions and revisions: Toraja culture and the tourist gaze," *American Ethnologist* 17: 91-110.

Yamamoto Michiko. 1993. *Deyo ka, Nippon, onna 31 sai: Amerika, Chûgoku o iku* [Shall I leave Japan? A woman of thirty-one travels to America and China]. Tokyo: Kôdansha.

Yamanaka Hayairi. 1992. *Imêji no "rakuen"* ["Paradise" in images]. Tokyo: Chikuma Shobô.

Yamashita Shinji. 1986. "Ujung Pandang no Toraja shakai: Indoneshia chihô toshi kenkyû" [The Toraja community in Ujung Pandang: a study of a regional city in Indonesia], *Tônanajia Kenkyû* [Southeast Asia Research] 23: 419-38.

Yamashita Shinji. 1988. *Girei no seijigaku: Indoneshia, Toraja no dôtaiteki minzokushi* [The politics of ritual: A dynamic ethnography of the Toraja of Indonesia]. Tokyo: Kôbundô.

Yamashita Shinji. 1992. "'Gekijô kokka' kara 'ryokôsha no rakuen' e: 20 seiki Bali ni okeru 'geijutsu, bunka shisutemu' to shite no kankô" [From "theater state" to "tourist paradise": Tourism as an "art-culture system" in twentieth-century Bali], *Minzoku Hakubutsukan Kenkyû Hôkoku* [The Bulletin of the National Museum of Ethnology], 17: 1-32.

Yamashita Shinji. 1993. "Rakuen Bari no enshutsu: Kankô jinruigakuteki oboekaki" [Staging Paradise in Bali: Notes from the anthropology of tourism], pp. 139-52 in *Oseania 2: Kindai ni ikiru* [Oceania Vol. 2: Living in modernity]. Shimizu Yasutoshi and Yoshioka Masanori, eds.Tokyo: The University of Tokyo Press.

Yamashita Shinji. 1994a. "Rekishi to shinwa: Rekishi jinruigaku no kanôsei" [History and myth: The possibility of historical anthropology]. *Kokubungaku*, 39: 28-35.

Yamashita Shinji. 1994b. "Minzoku bunka no katarikata" [Narrating ethnic culture], *Kikan Minzokugaku* [Ethnological Quarterly] 68: 57.

Yamashita Shinji. 1994c. "Manipulating ethnic tradition: Funeral ceremony, tourism, and television among the Toraja of Sulawesi," *Indonesia* 58: 69-82.

Yamashita Shinji. 1995a. "Ôsoprakushî kara ôsodokishî e: Gendai Bari shûkyôron oboekaki" [From orthopraxy to orthodoxy: a note on religious change in contemporary Bali, Indonesia], pp. 39-54 in *Shûkyô, minzoku, dentô: Ideorogîronteki kôsatsu* [Religion, nation, and tradition: ideological considerations]. Sugimoto, Yoshio, ed. Nagoya: Nanzan Anthropological Institute.

Yamashita Shinji. 1995b. "Dentô no sôsa: Indoneshia Toraja ni okeru kankô kaihatsu to 'shûkyô no saisei'" [Manipulating ethnic tradition: The development of tourism among the Toraja of Indonesia and the "revival of religion"], pp. 269-92 in *Ajia ni okeru shûkyôno saisei: Shûkyôteki keiken no poritikusu* [The religious revivals in Asia: Politics of religious experience]. Tanabe Shigeharu, ed. Kyoto: Kyoto Daigaku Gakujitsu Shuppankai [Kyoto University Academic Press].

Yamashita Shinji. 1995c. "Furontia no minzoku bunka: Indoneshia no chôsa kara" [Ethnic culture on the frontier: An Indonesian case], *Sôgôteki Chiiki Kenkyû* [Integrated regional research] (Kyoto University, Center for Southeast Asian Studies), 8: 32-38.

Yamashita, Shinji. 1995d. "Culture in the context of tourism: The interplay of national, regional and global perspectives," pp. 105-14 in *Regional Cooperation and Culture in Asia-Pacific*. Khien Theeravit and Grant B. Stillman eds. Tokyo: United Nations University Press.

Yamashita Shinji. 1996a. "Kankô jinruigaku annai" [Guide to the anthropology of tourism] pp. 4-15 in *Kankô jinruigaku* [The anthropology of tourism]. Yamashita Shinji ed. Tokyo: Shinyôsha.

Yamashita Shinji. 1996b. "'Rakuen' no sôzô: Bali ni okeru kankô to dentô no saikôchiku" [The creation of "paradise": Tourism and the reinvention of tradition in Bali], pp. 104-12 in *Kankô jinruigaku* [The anthropology of tourism]. Yamashita Shinji, ed. Tokyo: Shinyôsha.

Yamashita Shinji. 1996c. "'Kanibaru Tsuâzu': Papuanyûginea, Sepikkugawa ryûiki no kankô" ["Cannibal Tours": Tourism in the Sepik River region of Papua New Guinea], pp. 141-49 in *Kankô jinruigaku* [The anthropology of tourism]. Yamashita Shinji, ed. Tokyo: Shinyôsha.

Yamashita Shinji. 1996d. "Kankô no jikan, kankô no kukan: Atarashii chikyû no ninshiki" [Tourist time, tourist space: A new way of seeing the world], pp. 99-115 in *Iwanami kôza gendai shakaigaku 6: Jikan to kukan no shakaigaku* [Iwanami Series in Contemporary sociology, 6: The sociology of time and space]. Tokyo: Iwanami Shoten.

Yamashita Shinji. 1996e. "Minami e! Kita e!" [To the South! To the North!], pp. 1-28 in *Iwanami kôza bunkajinruigaku 7: Idô no minzokushi* [Iwanami Series in Cultural Anthropology, 7: The ethnography of migration]. Tokyo: Iwanami Shoten.

Yamashita Shinji. 1996f. "Minami e: Bali kankônaka no nihonjin" [To the South! The Japanese and tourism in Bali], pp. 31-59 in *Iwanami kôza bunkajinruigaku 7: Idô no minzokushi* [Iwanami Series in Cultural Anthropology, 7: The ethnography of migration]. Tokyo: Iwanami Shoten.

Yamashita Shinji. 1997. "Kankô kaihatsu to chiikiteki aidentiti no sôshutsu" [The development of tourism and the creation of regional identity], pp. 107-24 in *Iwanami kôza: Kaihatsu to bunka 3: Hankaihatsu no shisô* [Iwanami Series in Development and Culture, 3: Ideas of resistance to development]. Tokyo: Iwanami Shoten.

Yamashita Shinji. 1998a. "Bunka jinruigaku o vâshonappu suru" [Upgrading cultural anthropology], pp. 136-51 in *Bunka jinruigaku no susume* [Invitation to cultural anthropology]. Funabiki Takeo, ed. Tokyo: Chikuma Shobô.

Yamashita, Shinji. 1998b. "Kankô o yomi toku jûsatsu" [Ten books on understanding tourism], *Ronza* (June): 274-79.

Yamashita Shinji. 1998c. "Shohyô: Ôta Yoshinobu sha, *Toransupojishon no shisô*" [Review of Ôta, Yoshinobu, *The idea of transposition*], *Minzokugaku Kenkyû* [Japanese Journal of Ethnology] 63: 121-25.

Yamashita Shinji. ed. 1996. *Kankô jinruigaku* [The anthropology of tourism]. Tokyo: Shinyôsha.

Yamashita Shinji and Kagami Haruya. 1995. "Balitô Punripuran mura: Kankô kaihatsu no saizensen" [Penglipuran Village: The frontier of the development of tourism in Bali], *Kikan Minzokugaku* [Ethnological Quarterly] 73: 100-07.

Yamashita Shinji and Yamamoto Matori eds. 1997. *Shokuminchishugi to bunka: Jinruigaku no pâsupekutiv* [Colonialism and culture: An anthropological perspective]. Tokyo: Shinyôsha.

Yamashita, Shinji, Kadir H. Din and J.S. Eades eds. 1997. *Tourism and Cultural Development in Asia and Oceania*. Bangi, Malaysia: Penerbit Universiti Kebangsaan Malaysia.

Yanagita Kunio. 1956. *Yukiguni no haru* [Spring in Snow Country]. Tokyo: Kadokawa Shoten.

Yanagita Kunio. 1975. *Tôno monogatari* [Tales of Tôno]. Tokyo: Kadokawa Shoten.

Yanagita Kunio. 1976 [1927]. *Seinen to gakumon* [Youth and learning]. Tokyo: Iwanami Shoten.

Yoshida Teigo ed. 1994. *Bali tômin* [The Bali Islanders]. Tokyo: Kôbundô.

Yoshimi, Toshiya. 1992. *Hakurankai no seijigaku* [The politics of exhibitions]. Tokyo: Chûôkôronsha.

Index

Acciaioli, G. 44
accommodation 74
acculturation 9, 10, 144-45
Adams, K. 122
adat 49; see also custom
Adia Wirattmadja 69
administrative villages 49, 70, 110; see also villages
advertising 18, 26, 72, 88
Africa 29
agama 57, 120, 127
aging 4
agriculture 7
AIDS 4
Ainu 9
Airu (I'll) 93
Aka 127
Akasaka, N. 140
alienation 18
alternative tourism 102
Aluk To Dolo' 66, 71, 120-21
America 5, 7, 16, 83, 92, 129
American Anthropological Association 6
American Indians 132
Amlapura 66
Amsterdam 5
Anak Agung Gede Ngurah Mandera 41
ancestors 68, 71, 106, 120, 131
Andaman Islanders 7
Anderson, B. 21
Andilolo', J. 114
angel dance 34, 36
animism 71, 120
anthropology 4, 6, 14; history of 6; of tourism 5, 8
Appadurai, A. 4, 21, 151
Arabia 29
Arata, M. 145
Argonauts of the Western Pacific 7
art, Balinese 8
art-culture system 38, 40, 44, 134
Artaud, A. 34

Asia Pacific 42
assimilation 9, 10
Atkinson, J. 70
Australia 97, 100, 129
Australians xiii, xix, 129
authenticity 18-19, 31, 33, 38, 40, 73-74, 99, 104, 122, 133-34, 147
azan 63

babi guling 78
Badui 66
Badung 25, 103
bale banjar 84, 108
Bali xiii-xvi, xix, 7-11, 24-101, 145-46, 148, 150; and history 24-33; and Hinduism in 57-71; and 42-56; and Japan 87-101; and performance 33-40; and tourism 72-86, 102-10;
Bali aga 110;
Bali Arts Center 46
Bali Arts Festival xv, 46, 48, 82, 85
Bali Beach Hotel 52
Bali Hotel 29, 80
Bali Post 64-65
Bali-balihan 80
Bali: The Last Paradise 26
Balinese 8
Balinization 33
Bandem 83
Bangli 26, 102, 105, 108, 110
banjar 83-84
Banjar Tengah 83
bargaining 130
baris 35
baris gede 80
barong 34-35, 58, 75, 79, 87, 89
baseball 5
Basque region 150
Batak 43
Batavia 26; see also Jakarta
Bateson, G. 30-31, 37, 39
batik 64, 78, 134, 150
Batu Kila 116

Index

law 28, 49, 50-51, 70; see also *adat*
lawar 79
layout, of villages 106
Leach, E. 17
Legian Avenue 104
legong 34, 79
Leicester 16
leisure 17, 88
life styles 9
liminality 17
Linnekin, J. 145
lion dance 87
Listibiya 48
Liverpool 14, 16
lobsters 79, 89
localization 149, 151
lomba 46; *desa* 50; *desa adat* 50, 64;
    seka terna 64; *subak* 50; *subak
    abian* 50, 64
Lombok 92, 100, 103
London 5, 15-16, 21, 82, 97
lontara 63
Loughborough 16
Lovina 103
Lumanjang 60

ma'badong 117-18, 121
MacCannell, D. 4, 15, 18, 40, 74, 76,
    99
Madagascar 70
magariya 140, 142
Majapahit 28
Makale 114
Makassar 29, 113, 119, 126
Malay peninsula 119
Malaysia 54, 143
Malinowski, B. 6
Manchester 14
mandala wisata 52
Mandhara Giri 60-61
Manila 98
marakka 117
marriage 87, 94-98, 101
Marshon, K. 30
Marx, K. 18
Mas 74, 89
mass tourism 108
Matsuda, M. 87
Matsui, Y. 150
Matsuzaki, K. 143
Maugham, W. Somerset 7

Maya 71
McKean, P. 36, 74
McPhee, C. 30, 39-40
Mead, M. 7, 30-33, 35, 37, 39-40, 69
meaning 4
Mecca 61
media 4
Meiji enlightenment 141
Mekar Sari 83
mélange, global 5
Mengkendek 113-14, 116
merantau 119
Merina 70
metanarratives 9
Mexico 6, 79, 143
mie goreng 79
migration 6, 21, 99, 103, 118, 119, 120-
    22, 124, 148, 151
Minanga 113, 117, 123
Minangkabau 100
Ministry of Education and Culture 44-
    46
Ministry of Religion 57-58, 120
Ministry of the Interior 51
Ministry of Tourism, Post and
    Telecommunications 46
missionaries 129
Miyauchi, K. 8-9, 12
Miyoshi, K. 144
models 88
modernity 9-11, 13, 18, 40, 65, 148
Moeran, B. 19, 92
monkey dance 35
Monogatari Kura 142
Moon, O. 8
morals 62
Morocco 5
Morse, R. 146
mortuary rituals 17
Moscow 29, 30
mountains 61
Mozart, W. 129
museums 38, 140, 143
mushioi 142
music 30, 33-34, 39, 72, 77, 95, 107,
    117, 146
music halls 16
Muslims 57
Myanmar 127

Nagafuchi, Y. 28

Index